When Good People

Behave Badly

Management Dilemmas

How often do you wish you could turn to a panel of experts to guide you through tough management situations? The Management Dilemmas series provides just that. Drawn from the pages of *Harvard Business Review*, each insightful volume poses several perplexing predicaments and shares the problem-solving wisdom of leading experts. Engagingly written, these solutions-oriented collections help managers make sound judgment calls when addressing everyday management dilemmas.

Other books in the series

When Change Comes Undone

When Marketing Becomes a Minefield

When Good People

Behave Badly

Harvard Business School Press

Boston, Massachusetts

The *Harvard Business Review* articles in this collection are available as
individual reprints. Discounts apply to quantity purchases. For information and ordering please contact Customer Service, Harvard Business
School Publishing, Boston, MA 02163. Telephone (617) 783-7500 or
(800) 988-0886, 8 A.M. to 6 P.M. Eastern Time, Monday through Friday.
Fax (617) 783-7555, 24 hours a day. E-mail: custserv@hbsp.harvard.edu

Library of Congress Cataloging-in-Publication Data
Management dilemmas. When good people behave badly.
        p.   cm. — (Management dilemmas series)
    ISBN 1-59139-504-6

1. Problem employees—Problems, exercises, etc. 2. Labor discipline—
Problems, exercises, etc. I. Title: When good people behave badly. II.
Harvard Business School Press. III. Series.
HF5549.5.E42M35 2004
658.3´045—dc22

                                                           2004000445

The paper used in this publication meets the minimum requirements of the
American National Standard for Information Sciences—Permanence of
Paper for Printed Library Materials, ANSI Z39.48-1992.

CONTENTS

Introduction

Think of the best manager you've ever known. Ever wonder what made him or her so good at the job? If you're like most people, the managers you admire most are not remembered as brilliant strategists nor as masters of the budgeting process. No, whatever their strengths and failings in these critical management skills, our role models stand head and shoulders above the rest in one critical respect: their ability to manage people.

Great managers know how to get the most out of their teams. They know how to inspire their most highly skilled people to work toward a common, ambitious goal. They even know how to motivate and mentor underperforming employees who, in other managers' hands, might never achieve excellence. And, perhaps most difficult of all, they know how to deal with their problem employees—those people who deserve to keep their jobs based on measures of personal productivity, but who make it difficult for those around them to succeed.

How do some business leaders learn to manage problem employees so well? Not, for the most part, in the classroom. There are, of course, many distinguished business school professors teaching courses in organizational behavior, and their lessons are always informed by a rich body of research into human psychology and sociology. But these scholars would be the first to admit that people management, more than the management of any other resource, is an inexact science. The "right answers" nearly always come down to highly subjective calls. Therefore, the ability of practicing managers to deal, day in and day out, with the people issues that confront them is much less a question of having the right models and clinical findings at their fingertips, and much more a matter of developing good judgment. That's why, at *Harvard Business Review,* we devote so many of our case studies to human resource dilemmas.

Judgment Calls

Aimed at helping managers develop their problem-solving skills and learn to exercise sound managerial judgment, *Harvard Business Review* Case Studies are uniquely designed to explore the more subjective areas of management. In every issue of the magazine, a new case presents a common managerial dilemma, and then asks several expert commentators to weigh in with advice on how the problem might be resolved. The dilemma is illustrated by a short story that is fictional—yet all too real for untold numbers of managers. Nearly always, the commentators are at odds with each other in terms of the solutions they recommend. And that is the point, really. A dilemma wouldn't be a dilemma, after all, if all reasonable parties could agree on the path forward.

For the magazine's quarter of a million readers—most of them executives in large organizations—the case goes beyond being a good read. It's a chance for readers to exercise their managerial faculties and to match wits with the experts. Typically, readers study the story line, and then pause to consider what advice they would offer to the protagonist. Only then do they go on to read the commentaries, looking for the words of wisdom that best align with their own views. Indeed, sometimes their point of view isn't represented by the commentators, which may explain why the Case Study generates more than its share of letters to the editor: "Here's the perspective that all of your so-called experts missed!"

Harvard Business Review editors relish these kinds of letters because they're evidence that we're fulfilling our goal as a magazine. That goal, which is shared by all the units of Harvard Business School Publishing, is to improve the practice of management. And what could be more perfectly aligned with that mission than the HBR case study? It yields improvement through practice.

At its best, the case also takes on issues where that practice is urgently needed. As editors, we try to select topics for cases that are not only open to controversy but also of growing importance. Sometimes, the reason there is no best answer to a problem is that the problem is too new to have been researched thoroughly or considered from enough angles.

What Will You Do?

In this collection, we hope you'll find insightful advice to help you make the right call in tough situations. So where should you start? You could, of course, begin with the first and read them in order. But a quick overview might help you to select those of greatest interest or relevance to your own organization. Here, title by title, are the key issues raised by the cases and some hints as to how the commentators respond.

Bob's Meltdown

This case, written by former HBR executive editor Nick Carr, hits the topic of this collection dead center. It portrays a good person behaving badly, pure and simple. Bob Dunn, a senior vice president at Concord Machines, is under considerable pressure to produce near-term profits; the unit he heads up is new and service oriented, and the company's CEO sees its margins as Concord's salvation. But the business is in the midst of a downturn, and things haven't been going well. In fact, enough things have gone wrong in a row—a client situation blows up, his teenage son wrecks his car—that when Bob gets what he views as a time- and resource-wasting request from the company's new vice president of knowledge management, he sees it as the last straw. The story, which features a shifting narrative voice, shows us the impact of his "meltdown"—a tray-throwing tantrum in the company cafeteria—on a range of colleagues, from the VP of knowledge management herself to the administrative employee who puts together Bob's PowerPoint presentations.

It's a regrettable lapse of decorum, as even Bob realizes on some level. So how should the CEO respond? Commentator Nicole Gardner, head of human resources at Mercer Management Consulting, thinks his biggest problem may not be Bob. While not letting Bob off the hook completely, she says that the new VP's decision to "suddenly launch an initiative that would distract the business units was unconscionable." On the other hand, Victor Newman of Pfizer Pharmaceuticals cautions that the VP of knowledge management, having been on the receiving end of Bob's abuse, might have a legal case against the company. He advises a weeklong leave of absence for Bob, during which time Bob will agree to see his doctor. Kathleen Ligocki of Ford Motor Company believes that Bob must make a public apology, but should be given another chance. The CEO, she says, is responsible for creating the conditions that made some kind of clash inevitable. Robert Kramer of the Conference Board agrees, citing the "wide divide between corporate headquarters and the business units," and lays out a path forward if the company truly wants pragmatic executives like Bob to embrace the kind of initiative the VP of knowledge management is pushing.

A Question of Character

Appearing in the September–October 1999 issue, this case, by former HBR editor-in-chief Suzy Wetlaufer, addresses a question that had been much in the news for over a year. It was in January of 1998 that the world learned of President Bill Clinton's extramarital relationship with "that woman," Monica Lewinsky. At the height of a boom economy, many wished Clinton's indiscretions hadn't come to light. What did it have to do, they suggested, with how good a president he was? The same question is at the heart of this story: Should it really matter to the company's employees and board of directors that the leader—in this case Joe Ryan, CEO of a cosmetics company—cheats on his wife?

Mitch Kapor, the founder and former CEO of Lotus Development Corporation, and his wife Freada Kapor Klein, a former human resource executive, think it does. The CEO's behavior, they say, has a substantial impact on the business's success. But termination would be unfair. Instead, they say the company's board should offer help in the form of executive coaching. Burke Stintson, in public relations at AT&T, suggests a compelling tactic for getting the CEO's supporters to see the light: Prepare a report in the form of a damaging newspaper exposé, to show what would happen if the full story got out. A third commentator, Patrick Carnes, treats people who have addiction disorders, and suggests that one might be at the root of this case. And Daryl Koehn, a professor of business ethics, notes that if we continually rationalize questionable behavior outside the office, there is nothing to stop us from explaining away corrupt behavior at work.

What a Star—What a Jerk

Sarah Cliffe's case study focuses on the management challenge posed by a top-performing salesperson who also happens to be nasty and bullying to subordinates. One of the few HBR cases presented in epistolary form, this one consists of an ongoing e-mail exchange between an executive new to a company and a former colleague at the consulting firm she recently left. Her problem employee is one Andy Zimmerman, who regularly "reams out" administrative and other staff, yet is smart, efficient, and the best she's got in terms of pure performance.

Should Andy be punished for his behavior in some way? Sloan School professor Mary Rowe is more inclined to reward him on those occasions when his behavior is good. Either way, she notes, the key is consistency: "The worst thing a supervisor can do is to sometimes reward and sometimes punish unacceptable behavior." Chuck McKenzie, a senior vice president at Oppenheimer Funds who has managed an Andy or two in his time, agrees it would be foolish to fire him. He notes that the group may have to learn to cope with "true diversity"—the wide range of personalities the business world has to offer. Executive coach Kathy Jordan accuses Jane, Andy's manager, of being far too passive. Jordan believes that Jane needs to explain in no uncertain terms that good numbers are not enough, and that Andy's job depends on his ability to manage relationships with colleagues professionally. And finally, psychologist and consultant James Waldroop advises Jane on how to stroke this extremely narcissistic man's ego and at the same time hammer him hard with critique.

When Your Star Performer Can't Manage

Linus Carver, the "problem employee" of this case written by Gordon Adler, is a man who can "in ten days, single-handedly, do the work of an entire development team." He can work for 15 hours without a break, and not miss a detail. He once went two days straight without leaving the office or sleeping. The problem is, as head of product development, he shouldn't have to be such a superman. He has the company's entire engineering and design staff reporting to him, if only he could learn to delegate—and trust his people to deliver. The case raises the broader question of how to handle brilliant, difficult individuals within an organization.

Yale management professor Victor Vroom suspects that Carver, the one-man band, might actually be unhappy in his managerial role. He urges the CEO to engage him in real dialogue—not simply advice-giving sessions—to find out. June Rokoff, a board member of two innovative software firms, tells the CEO to sit tight. There's no reason to "do something" with a manager who meets, she believes, "most of the requirements of the perfect product-development leader." David Olsen, president of the outerwear firm Patagonia (which resembles the company in the case) disagrees, saying "Vic has a bigger problem on his hands than he thinks." He needs to start working right away to create a culture that encourages innovation from everyone. And consultant David Burnham adds a suggestion about Carver's performance-based compensation. Why not make half of it contingent on his management of the team—to be measured by the diversity of ideas generated and by employee satisfaction levels?

Do Something—He's About to Snap

Eileen Roche, the HBR editor who authored this case, had the sense that her timing was spectacularly unlucky. Between the time she invited the commentators and the time they drafted their responses, one of the four actually had an incident of lethal workplace violence occur in his organization. The case had barely appeared in print when two more incidents hit the national news in quick succession. Quite unintentionally, the case was topical—and somewhat controversial in that it depicts an employee who poses no real performance problems other than giving his colleagues the creeps.

James Alan Fox, a criminal justice professor at Northeastern University, doubts that Max Dyer, the paranoid loner in the case, is actually a serious threat. "Treating Max like a ticking time bomb can actually do much more harm than good," he points out. Steve Kaufer of the Workplace Violence Research Institute concurs, saying that Max's manager needs to stop walking on eggshells around him. What he needs is some constructive counseling on his behavior. Business professors Christine Pearson and Christine Porath see in the situation not a life-threatening maniac, but an uncivil person, surrounded by incivility—none of which should be tolerated. Only Ronald Schouten (whose employer, Massachusetts General Hospital, had just experienced the on-the-job murder of a doctor) cautions Max's manager about the consequences of failing to act.

When Salaries Aren't Secret

John Case's provocative story about a departing employee's parting shot is something few readers will probably ever experience, but all can have fun imagining. What would happen if, in your e-mail box one morning, you and all your coworkers received a list of all company employees—and their salaries?

Victor Sim of Prudential Insurance knows exactly what would happen, because until recently it was required by law that his mutual insurance company post the names and salaries of all employees making more than $60,000. While not wishing such disclosure on any company, he advises companies to get their houses in order by creating compensation systems with defined pay grades. Dennis Bakke, CEO of AES Corporation, opines that, when people know each others' salaries, it "leads to a healthier work environment." But Ira Kay of compensation consulting firm Watson Wyatt cautions against too much openness, noting that "internal equity usually clashes with paying people their external market value." Finally, the author of *Winning the Talent Wars,* Bruce Tulgan, proposes a radical new approach to pay: negotiating employees' pay just like contractors'—project by project, and according to the value of the work being done.

Just-in-Case Knowledge

There's a theme, of course, running through all the case studies collected here. They all deal with what happens to group dynamics when one person behaves badly. If you're a manager, you've probably had your share of such personality and behavior issues. You might even look upon these cases with some measure of self-recognition—or perhaps relief that "there but for the grace of God go I." There's another theme at work here as well: that so much of good people management comes down to subjective judgment calls, made in very specific contexts.

We could even make the case that today's manager needs a greater capacity for such judgment than ever before. The workplace of the 21st century is one that tolerates—even invites—more employee assertiveness. We see less hierarchy; more recognition of the need for work/life balance; a growing recognition of persistent patterns of unfairness and of the need for diversity; the increased threat of legal action for unjustified dismissal—the list goes on.

So many emerging issues, so many judgment calls. It's our hope that, by thinking through the dilemmas in this collection, you'll be better prepared to make your own.

Bob's Meltdown

Executive Summary

Annette Innella is just coming into the lunchroom at Concord Machines when Bob Dunn starts screaming at her. After throwing his lunch tray against the wall, he stomps out, leaving Annette stunned.

Naturally, Annette, the new senior VP for knowledge management, is beside herself. She knows her proposal to establish a cross-functional knowledge management committee is progressive thinking for this old-line manufacturer, but Bob's reaction is totally over the line. If Bob stays, she goes—that's all there is to it.

Bob is contrite, but he's under a lot of pressure. The general manager of the Services Group, he's just returned from a two-week trip around the globe to gear up his troops to beat revenue targets again, despite shrinking budgets and hiring freezes. And what does he see when he gets back? An e-mail from Annette requesting that two of his best people devote half their time to what he calls her "idiotic" Knowledge Protocols Group. He's carrying the company on his back, and she's throwing this nonsense at him.

Graphics specialist Paula Chancellor is surprised. Sure, Bob's gruff, but his staff loves him, and he's the only one of the big shots who ever talks to her. But HR director Nathan Singer is incensed; Bob's never been a team player, Singer complains, and it's time he learned a lesson.

CEO Jay Nguyen is in a bind. Bob is his top manager; he brings in all the money. And even though future revenues are going to have to come from somewhere else, Jay is not totally behind Annette's initiative in the current business climate. He can't afford to lose Bob. But if he reins in Annette, it will look like he's condoning Bob's outburst. What should he do?

Four commentators offer advice in this fictional case study.

Annette Innella, Vice President, Knowledge Management: It was the most humiliating experience of my life. I knew Bob Dunn didn't see eye-to-eye with me, but I would never have imagined he'd attack me the way he did. I felt completely exposed and violated. Even now, nearly two days later, I'm angry and upset—I can hardly concentrate on my job.

The morning had actually started off quite well. Alex Brigham, one of the most respected consultants on knowledge management, had flown in from San Francisco to meet with me and go over our situation here at Concord Machines. It was an extremely productive meeting—Alex was surfacing all sorts of out-of-the-box ideas—and we decided to continue it over lunch. We had just come into the company cafeteria when out of nowhere someone starts yelling. At first, I had no idea what was going on. Then I realized that it was Bob Dunn—he was at a table by the door, just a few feet from me—and that it was me he was screaming at. I was stunned, speechless. I just stood there while he went on and on, ranting about how I didn't know anything and how I was wrecking the company. It was very personal. Then he stood up and threw his lunch tray against the wall and stormed out, passing within a foot or two of me. I was scared. I sincerely thought he might do something physical.

Needless to say, I couldn't eat after that. Alex kindly escorted me out of the cafeteria and back to my office. The rest of the day is a blur. At some point after Alex left for the airport, Nathan Singer, the head of HR, came by and talked with me for a long time, and then Jay Nguyen, our CEO, called me from Toronto, where he was attending a conference. But to be honest, I can't really remember much of what either Nathan or Jay said. Obviously, though, they were both extremely upset by Bob's outburst.

I knew when I started here six months ago that I'd have a tough time. Concord Machines is an old-line manufacturer that's very set in its ways. They don't really understand that we're in a fundamentally new economy now and that a company's knowledge is its greatest competitive asset. Everyone here is still locked in their business and functional silos; there's no cross-unit teaming, no sharing. Jay told me he wanted me to shake things up, and that's what I've been trying to do. The Friday before this happened, Jay had okayed my proposal to establish a knowledge management committee—the Knowledge Protocols Group—that would bring together the best and the brightest from every unit to create a strategy and set an example for the rest of the company. I guess that's what set Bob off. He must have viewed it as an encroachment on his turf—his precious little Services Division.

I've come to believe that there are two types of people in business: the constructive and the destructive. Destructive people can succeed for a while if they're smart and competent and energetic, but in the end they'll do far more harm than good to an organization. I sensed from the start that Bob Dunn was a destructive person, and now I'm sure of it. He may be an important part of Concord Machines' past, but he's certainly not part of its future. I don't think Jay has any choice at this point but to let him go. I know I can't stay if he stays.

Robert Dunn, Senior Vice President and General Manager, Services: I'm not making any excuses—what I did was totally unacceptable—but you have to understand I'd been under a heck of a lot of pressure. We were two weeks into the fourth quarter, the company was behind budget on both revenue and income, and so of course everyone was looking to Services to make up the shortfall. They still call Concord Machines a manufacturer, but it doesn't make money on product sales anymore.

All of our margin and most of our growth are coming from service contracts and spare parts sales—thanks to me and my people. Three years ago, when they put me in charge of the unit, we barely even had a services business; it was an afterthought. I cleaned the organization out and rebuilt it from scratch. I overhauled all our processes, brought in and trained a crackerjack sales force, expanded successfully into Europe and Asia. This year, Services will bring in nearly half of the company's revenue and virtually all of its profit. Hell, Services is Concord Machines.

At the start of the quarter, Jay called me into his office and laid it on the line. He told me, first, that I was going to have to beat my revenue target and, second, that a hiring freeze had been put into effect and, third, that they were going to take a quarter million out of my marketing budget. So I was in a vise, as usual. But I didn't whine about it. I just said, "Okay, I'll get it done." First thing I had to do was clear: rally the troops. I hopped on a plane, and I did the circuit—London, Paris, and Munich; then Taiwan and Singapore; and around to Phoenix and Dallas. I got home, and before I'd even had a chance to kiss the wife, the guys in London call me back. A big client in Glasgow is wavering about signing a contract extension, and they need me to help clinch the deal. Fine. I take the next flight. Then, while I'm in Scotland, I get a hysterical message from my wife. Our son, Gregg, has been in a car accident. Everyone's fine, but my car—a new Explorer—is totaled, and Gregg's been arrested for driving under the influence and possession of alcohol as a minor. It's a nightmare. When I finally get back, last Friday night, I have to deal with that. I'm the last person to use my personal life to make excuses for my job, but face it: Stress is stress. I'm human like everybody else.

Then comes the last straw. I get into the office Monday morning at seven, and I've got an e-mail from Annette Innella—this woman that Jay brought in six months ago to be in charge of "knowledge manage-

---

So when Annette came into the lunchroom with another of her high-priced consultants and gave me that patronizing little smile of hers, I just lost it.

---

ment," whatever the hell that means—saying that she's launching something called a Knowledge Protocols Group. And, get this, she wants each department head to assign two of their "most talented lieutenants" (that's a direct quote) to this KPG team. She says that they should be freed up enough from their operating duties to devote at least half their time to KPG. I nearly threw my computer through the window. I mean, they're squeezing my division to save the company's butt, and then they throw this nonsense at us. Give me a break.

So when Annette came into the lunchroom with another of her high-priced consultants and gave me that patronizing little smile of hers, I just lost it. I mean, she knows nothing about this business. She's a waste of space—a corporate black hole. I really have no idea why Jay hired her in the first place. It was a huge mistake. So, yeah, I'm sorry for blowing up; it was a truly stupid move. But I'm carrying this company on my back, and that has to count for something.

Nathan Singer, Senior Vice President, Human Resources: We have a set of values in this company that we spent a lot of time creating, and I take those values very seriously. One of our values is entitled "Respect." This is what it says: "We value the unique and diverse talents of our coworkers, and we treat them at all times with respect and consideration." Say whatever you want about Annette—I personally think she's a breath of fresh air around here—but one thing is crystal clear. Bob Dunn acted in a way that was totally inconsistent with our company values. Screaming at a colleague in public and acting in a violent and threatening manner are outside the bounds of acceptable workplace behavior. If Bob is allowed to get away with this, it will undermine our values completely. I mean, who is going to take them seriously if he gets away with just a slap on the wrist?

Frankly, Bob Dunn has never taken this company's culture seriously. He wasn't onboard when we developed our mission and values, and I'd go so far as to say he treated the entire process with contempt. Of course, that's typical for Bob. He runs Services like it's his own private kingdom, like it's separate from the rest of the company. He routinely ignores or even insults the other executives here, particularly those in corporate roles like myself. He hasn't even returned my calls about this incident. He's just not a team player, and as Jay has made clear on many occasions, everyone in this company is part of the team. I know Bob gets results, but results aren't the only thing that matters. Bob's a dinosaur, when you get down to it, and though I'd like to give him the benefit of the doubt, it wouldn't surprise me if one of the reasons he attacked Annette is because she's a woman. I think he feels threatened.

Paula Chancellor, Graphics Specialist: I was sitting in the cafeteria eating a salad when Bob Dunn came in and sat down at my table. We all love Bob. He's gruff and has a temper, but he's a great guy. I mean, no other big shot at this company would even think about sitting down and having lunch with me—I'm just the anonymous person who cranks out their PowerPoint slides. Bob, though, makes it a point to know your name and to always ask how you're doing.

Anyway, I could tell he was in a bad mood that day. We said hi to each other, and then we just ate our lunches quietly. I was flipping through a magazine, kind of in my own world. Then all hell breaks loose. I hear Bob say, really loud, "You've got to be kidding me, right?" I look up, and at first I think he might be yelling at me—his face is bright red, he's really steaming, and I'm thinking, "What the heck did I do?"—and then I realize he's talking to that new knowledge management person. Her name's Annette, I think. There was a big memo about her when she joined.

Anyway, Annette—she's with this other guy I'd never seen before, with these trendy little glasses—she stops and just glares at Bob. "Excuse me?" she says. "Are you talking to me?" She is just totally shocked.

"This knowledge group thing," Bob says. "That has to be the stupidest idea I've ever heard in my life. It's

---

What a mess. Bob Dunn's the best manager I have. Hands down, the best. He understands the business, he works tirelessly, and he gets his people to do unbelievable things.

---

totally nuts. Do you have any clue what we do here? Have you looked at the numbers at all? You're going to screw up my whole damn operation when we can least afford it. You know what? You don't know the first thing about this company." Then he gets up and basically throws his lunch tray at the garbage can. There's food and trash all over the floor. He stomps out the door, and Annette's just standing there, in complete disbelief. It was crazy. People have been talking about it ever since. Everybody's wondering what Jay's going to do.

Jay Nguyen, President and CEO: What a mess. Bob Dunn's the best manager I have. Hands down, the best. He understands the business, he works tirelessly, and he gets his people to do unbelievable things. His people adore him, in fact—at least, those that have had the stamina to stick with him. This company would fall apart in five minutes without Bob. I know it, and he knows it.

But screaming at a colleague in the cafeteria? Throwing your tray? That's too much. I don't know where you draw the line, but that's definitely over it. The ironic thing is, I was probably just as angry about Annette's memo as Bob was. I hadn't given her a green light on setting up that group; I had just said it looked like a promising idea. And even that was an exaggeration—the last thing we need right now is for people to take their eyes off the bottom line. Now I'm really in a box. If I ask Annette to postpone the initiative, it'll look like I'm sanctioning Bob's behavior. And that's a message I can't send. Heck, I'd probably end up getting sued or something.

I brought Annette in because I was convinced that the company needed some fresh thinking. And I'm still convinced that's true. Our products are commodities at this point; we have to keep cutting manufacturing costs just to stay even. Bob's unit is making all the money, but that's eventually going to start flattening out, no matter how good a manager Bob is. We've got good people here, but we're not capturing their ideas. We need new products, new services, new strategies. I have my doubts about Annette—I'm not sure she fully understands the realities of the business we're in. But I have no doubt about the need to tap into our people's knowledge. No doubt at all.

I just don't know what to do. In some ways, I even feel I'm a little to blame here. I've been pushing Bob relentlessly. He's always seemed to thrive on pressure—the more work you give him, the more he wants. But maybe I went too far. Everybody has a breaking point.

How Should the CEO Respond to His Top Manager's Tantrum?

Four commentators offer expert advice.

➤ Nicole Gardner

Nicole Gardner is a vice president and the chief human resources officer at Mercer Management Consulting in Boston.

The big problem at Concord Machines is not Bob Dunn's behavior; it's Jay Nguyen's. Jay has clearly been struggling for some time with fundamental issues about the company and its future. But, equally clear, he has failed to share his thoughts and concerns with the rest of his top management team. No wonder Bob blew his stack—he's been put in an untenable position. His CEO is pushing him to focus relentlessly on the near term even as other executives are being urged to look out toward the horizon.

So, while Jay deals with the immediate mess, he needs to do some deep—and fast—thinking about where he's taking Concord Machines and what he wants from each member of his executive team. And then he needs to meet with the team and lay all his cards on the table. CEOs can't have secret agendas.

As for the current situation, healing the wounds is going to take careful listening and straight talk. Jay needs to sit down with Annette Innella, apologize for his own miscommunication, and then let her speak her mind, no matter how long it takes. She needs to know that he empathizes with her and shares her shock and disappointment at Bob's tantrum. But once she's had her say, Jay needs to deliver a hard message. Assuming that Annette knew about the financial pressures facing the company, her decision to suddenly launch an initiative that would distract the business units was unconscionable. And making it even worse was the fact that she used e-mail to deliver the message. In a company that reveres Bob Dunn because he connects personally with coworkers at all levels, delivering a sensitive announcement to colleagues over a computer screen is a cultural faux pas of the first order. Annette needs to understand that she made big errors.

It may be that Annette is, in fact, the wrong person for the job at hand. If Jay truly has serious doubts about her capabilities, as he seems to, he's going to have to bite the bullet and guide her toward a decision to be reassigned or to leave the company. It may be possible to have a B-list person manage an effort that's already up and running, but when it comes to spearheading a new, critical initiative, you need nothing less than top tier talent. Jay may need to cut his losses with Annette.

As for Bob, he already understands that he made a big mistake. Jay needs to reinforce that message with him and make it clear that Bob needs to apologize to Annette—in person. More important, though, Jay needs to tell Bob how valuable he is to the company. Bob is too important to be allowed to feel alienated by this incident—or even to be distracted by it. And then Jay needs to change Bob's marching orders. He needs Bob to delegate day-to-day decisions and firefights to his lieutenants; Bob cannot, and should not, continue to do everything himself. (To free Bob up, Jay may have to cough up some money for new managerial talent.) And then Bob has to broaden his own perspective, to help Jay plot Concord Machines' future. For all his success, Bob's being wasted in his current role.

Finally, the company grapevine needs tending. People are buzzing about this incident, and its resolution needs to be communicated through the ranks. As soon as Bob has talked with Annette, Jay should ask him to sit down with Paula Chancellor and tell her, first, that his behavior in the cafeteria was completely inappropriate and, second, that he's patched things up with Annette. Paula will quickly spread the word. It would also be helpful for Bob and Annette to be seen working together cordially from time to time. With luck, that will happen naturally.

➤ Victor Newman

Victor Newman is the head of the European Pfizer Research University in Sandwich, England. He speaks frequently on the subjects of organizational learning and knowledge management.

Jay has already lost two days. He must now act very quickly to defuse the situation, and at every step of the way he must display the kind of behavior he wants his managers to emulate. Just as important as *what* he does is *how* he does it.

Jay's first priority should be to sit down with Nathan Singer and review the potential risks the company faces should Annette bring legal action for assault or harassment. Contingency plans need to be put in place immediately. Nathan should clear his schedule for review meetings with Jay at the beginning and end of each day until the problem is resolved.

Jay also must meet right away with Bob. He needs to explain to Bob the risks the company faces as a result of his actions, and he needs to get Bob to take a weeklong emergency leave of absence to deal with his family problems, handing over the reins of Services to his second in command. During this week, Bob should have a full physical examination with the company doctor—and he should have no contact with Annette whatsoever. Jay needs to call Bob every day during his week off, expressing the company's concern for his family's and his own well-being. During these conversations, Jay himself needs to apologize for his own errors—for pushing Bob too hard and for failing to communicate clearly. That will help Bob become comfortable with the thought of apologizing to Annette.

Indeed, Jay's overarching goal should be to create the conditions for a meeting between Annette and Bob in which they listen to each other's point of view, develop empathy for each other, and renegotiate their relationship. A skilled counselor should be brought in to interview each of them and design the process for their reconciliation. At the same time, Jay should have Nathan develop severance packages for Annette and Bob in case they are unable to bridge their differences.

Jay also needs to do some soul-searching. What might he have done to avoid this situation? At the very least, he should have had a business continuity plan. That would have highlighted the risk of loading too much responsibility for profit generation onto any one person. Such a plan would have forced Bob to develop an explicit delegation strategy for developing his subordinates. Bob is locked into the heady, self-reinforcing adrenaline cycle of expert power. He loves being the deus ex machina who flies in to save the day. This cycle needs to be broken. Bob's busyness, not market conditions, may be the real constraint on Services' growth.

As for Annette, Jay should have given her a thorough orientation to the business, covering the company's entire value chain, and had her schedule meetings with all the VPs and senior VPs to discuss their roles and collect their views on knowledge management. Most important, Jay should have required Annette to formulate a detailed strategy for engaging and involving her peers before she took any action.

Launching headquarters-sponsored initiatives is always dangerous. All such programs, I've learned, must be viewed and promoted in terms of business value. For people like Bob Dunn, "knowledge management" is a meaningless term; it makes sense only to the degree it can be shown to generate concrete value. If Annette's efforts are going to bear fruit, she needs to provide answers—in clear, everyday language—to the three crucial questions that every employee will immediately ask: Why are we doing this? What's in it for me? What do I do now?

It's ironic that Bob's Services organization is in itself a good example of how knowledge, when well managed, can differentiate even a commodity. If only Annette had made that connection, Bob might have been her greatest ally.

➤ Kathleen Ligocki

Kathleen Ligocki is the vice president for Canada, Mexico, and North American strategy at Ford in Dearborn, Michigan.

Wouldn't life be easier if people were perfect? And wouldn't business be simpler if operating pressures were perfectly balanced with strategic considerations? Then again, how much less interesting a manager's job would be!

Jay sowed the seeds for this confrontation himself. Obviously, he has not worked with his management team to develop integrated objectives and align priorities. Instead, he upped the pressure on Services, his one high-performing operating unit, and on Bob, its head, while unleashing Annette, an inexperienced VP, with a broad, strategic knowledge-management initiative. Each was blind to the other's perspective. Neither treated the other with the respect and consideration core to the company's values. Some kind of clash was inevitable.

Bob's behavior in the cafeteria was clearly inappropriate; the most objective observer, Paula Chancellor, indicated that Bob instigated the confrontation. Since his blowup was public, he owes Annette a public apology—one appropriate forum would be a meeting of Jay's direct reports. Bob's overreaction might be better understood if he could share some of his personal life pressures. Most would sympathize.

Bob is a crusty, experienced, capable line manager who may never enthusiastically buy in to the sort of corporate mission and value statements that can fit on laminated cards. He will provoke the eternal antagonism of corporate staff folks like Nathan Singer. And he'll never be able to generate the fresh thinking so obviously needed by the company. He does, however, keep the cash flowing to fund the future. More than that, he is loved by the troops, inspiring them to achieve "unbelievable things." His outburst appears to be without precedent, and I don't buy Nathan's speculation that it was motivated by sexual prejudice—if that were the case, Paula probably would have noted it. This is more a case of the veteran versus the newcomer. If Bob agrees to an open, honest apology, he should be given another chance.

I have more reservations about Annette. She lacks maturity and political savvy. Jay brought her into the company six months ago "to shake things up," but I'm surprised that she has not built bridges to key line colleagues like Bob. Even if Bob rebuffed her, she could have orchestrated discussions with her peers and with Jay to garner support for her ideas. Instead, she dismisses Bob with a simplistic view of "constructive and destructive" businesspeople. She discounts his experience and successful track record without trying to understand his contribution. Annette might even have defused the cafeteria outburst if, instead of freezing, she had said she was interested in Bob's concerns and would like to discuss them at his convenience. Coaching might help Annette develop more cool in the face of fire.

As a company under operating pressures, Concord Machines needs to balance its long-term strategic initiatives with current operating realities. Accordingly, Jay needs to work with Annette to sketch out the proper scope of the knowledge management initiative. A more focused pilot program might allow Annette to demonstrate the merit of her ideas and give her time to explain her longer-term vision to her peers.

But more broadly, Jay needs to open up discussion of strategic issues with all his senior managers. The commoditization of Concord Machines' manufacturing products, coupled with the decline of competitive advantage in the services sector—the business that's generating all the money—demands that the company rethink its portfolio before all sources of cash generation evaporate.

Finally, I believe the management team needs to work on diversity—not necessarily related to gender, but to thought and perspective. The differences within the leadership group might actually be a source of strength if they can be harnessed in a productive way.

➤ Robert J. Kramer

Robert J. Kramer is a principal researcher with the Conference Board in New York. He is the author of the Board's Organizing for Global Competitiveness *reports and* Post-Merger Organization Handbook.

If Jay Nguyen is really serious about knowledge management, then responding to this unfortunate situation on a purely interpersonal level—by taking Bob to the woodshed and finding a way to mollify Annette—will serve at best as a temporary fix. The event has exposed deep organizational fault lines—ones that exist at many companies, by the way—and Jay needs to recognize and address them if he's ever going to take Concord Machines in new directions.

First, there is clearly a wide divide between corporate headquarters and the business units. The unit managers see their corporate counterparts as irritating meddlers. The corporate executives see the unit heads as narrow-minded turf warriors.

Second, Concord Machines appears to have a culture of decentralized management, in which the business units have a great deal of power. This culture would conflict with any corporate initiative, especially one like knowledge management, which so intimately involves the businesses.

In this context, the launch of a knowledge management initiative raises fundamental questions. Should the effort be run by headquarters, or should the units—the knowledge creators and users—be in charge? Will the effort require cultural change, or can it be done within the existing culture? Unfortunately, Jay appears never to have asked these questions. Like many CEOs, he has chosen to ignore his company's organizational conflicts in the vain hope that they'll somehow resolve themselves.

Now, however, Jay has to act. He needs to lay the organizational groundwork necessary for a successful knowledge management program, focusing on four areas:

Structure. Since business unit support is essential, Jay needs to incorporate knowledge management into the work of the units. He should ask each business head to appoint a knowledge management leader and team. In addition, Jay should revise the corporate leadership role Annette currently plays, stressing the importance of collaborating with the units to define knowledge management for Concord Machines, determine its costs and benefits, develop objectives, and formulate plans for achieving them.

Processes. The company needs to establish two different sets of processes. The first are basic knowledge management procedures and support systems. The second are collaborative working relationships between corporate staff and line units and between the corporate knowledge management activity and the knowledge management teams in the units.

People. To wield authority, the leader of Concord Machines' overall knowledge management initiative needs a broad set of capabilities: technical knowledge, relationships with key company executives, facilitation skills, and enthusiasm for the project. Jay is going to have to decide whether Annette, a newcomer, possesses these attributes. If not, she should be reassigned or helped to find employment elsewhere, and a search should be initiated to find an effective replacement. At the same time, Nathan should oversee the creation of an incentive system, covering all key line and staff players, that encourages the kind of collaborative behavior necessary for knowledge management to take hold.

Communication. Writing a memo is not enough. Jay needs to get out in front of the troops to stress the importance of knowledge management to Concord Machines and underscore the need for the business units and the corporate staff to work together. And as a plan is formulated and implemented, he needs to continue to take a visible role, reinforcing his interest and support.

So far, Jay has failed this leadership test. If he doesn't get on the ball, a temper tantrum will be the least of his worries.

Originally published in January 2002

Reprint R0201A

A Question of Character

Executive Summary

For the most part, Glamor-a-Go-Go's board has been thrilled with CEO Joe Ryan's performance. Ryan, after all, had transformed the private-label cosmetics company into a retail powerhouse with flashy outlets form New York to Los Angeles. In addition to saving the company from bankruptcy shortly after his arrival in 1992, Ryan had made Glamor-a-Go-Go a fun and exciting place to work, increasing workers' wages and creating boundless opportunities for anyone willing to work hard and think out of the box. He had also brought more women and people of color on board. And he had made many employees wealthy, with generous stock giveaways and options for the most senior employees down to the most junior. Glamor-a-Go-Go's stock price had grown tenfold during Ryan's tenure.

But Ryan's personal affairs were beginning to call into question his leadership abilities. The local paper's gossip column recently ran a photo of Ryan—a married man—leaving a gala event with a beautiful young woman from the company, with the headline "Who's That Girl?" Indeed, rumors about Ryan's philandering were starting to take on a harsher edge. Some people believed his secretary left because Ryan had sexually harassed her. Others believed a mailroom employee had been promoted to factory supervisor because of her affair with the CEO.

Having warned Ryan several times about his alleged infidelities, the board is stuck. What should it do about Ryan's extracurricular behavior? Does Ryan's personal behavior even affect the company? Is what Ryan does outside the office the board's concern? Six commentators weigh in.

Roger Cushing was always the first person to arrive at Glamor-a-Go-Go's corporate headquarters. He needed the quiet of the early morning to get ready for the craziness of the day—and days at Glamor-a-Go-Go were always crazy. But *good* crazy, Roger reminded himself. The company had just opened its 120th store, and 15 more were in the works. Not only did customers love the Glamor-a-Go-Go formula—department store cosmetics at drugstore prices—but they also couldn't get enough of the company's "Girl Power" line of private-label cosmetics. No wonder sales and profits were skyrocketing. And even more frenetic growth was in sight—with a bold plan to take the company global within 18 months. As head of Glamor-a-Go-Go's marketing group, Roger himself was deeply involved in preparing for that giant leap.

And so he arrived at 6:30 every day. He often used the quiet of the morning for reading. There was the competition to keep tabs on, of course, but as an executive at a company catering to teenagers and 20-somethings, he knew he also had to stay on top of popular culture. So while he started with the *Wall Street Journal,* he quickly turned to *Women's Wear Daily* and about a half-dozen teen and fashion magazines that he relied on for spotting trends. He also did a quick check of several Web sites each day. And finally, Roger scanned the local paper. It was a typical suburban-city daily—heavy on restaurant openings and high school sports—which occasionally featured an article on the company.

The paper was usually a big booster of Glamor-a-Go-Go—the area's largest employer and a major advertiser in the Help Wanted section. The newspaper had, in fact, recently given glowing front-page coverage to the company's Girl Power rally, where several Texas politicians had exhorted hundreds of local teenagers to make the most of their lives through education. But there was no boosterism in the photograph that Roger spotted almost instantly at the top of the gossip column in the Lifestyles section that morning. It showed his boss, CEO Joe Ryan, accompanied by a beautiful, smiling young woman. "Who's That Girl?" was the headline. The caption read, "Glamor-a-Go-Go CEO Joe Ryan was part of the 100-plus crowd that attended the gala opening of Houston's newest steak house, Rarebits, Saturday night. He is pictured leaving the party with a friend [identity unknown]. Ryan and his wife, Michelle, were recently named cochairs of Families First, the Texas charity that supports educational programs to prevent child abuse."

"Ouch," Roger groaned, "that hurts." And Ryan's "friend" in the picture was hardly unidentified—at least to people within the company. She was Laura Sanders, a 25-year-old assistant manager in Glamor-a-Go-Go's human resources department. Roger closed the newspaper and shook his head. "How could Joe do this," he wondered out loud. "How could he do it *again?*"

Roger's thoughts were interrupted by the telephone. At this hour, he knew it could only be Carol Tomkins, a member of Glamor-a-Go-Go's board and Roger's close friend for years. Together, they had both watched Joe Ryan transform Glamor-a-Go-Go from a chain of 23 run-down stores selling discount makeup in southern suburbs into a retail powerhouse, with flashy outlets everywhere from New York to Los Angeles. Together, they had watched him demonstrate great vision, strategic thinking, leadership—and personal behavior that could only be called idiotic. For years, they had debated what to do about the Joe Ryan "character question." They had always concluded, with some trepidation, that it didn't matter—until now.

Roger had noticed that in-house rumors about Ryan's philandering had recently taken on a harsher edge. For years, most employees had laughed about his reputation for flirting with young female staffers. After all, Ryan was immensely popular. Not only had he saved the company from bankruptcy after he was hired in 1992, but he had made Glamor-a-Go-Go a fun and exciting place to work, increasing workers' wages and creating boundless opportunities for anyone willing to work hard and think out of the box. Beyond that, Ryan had delivered on his promise to diversify the workforce, bringing more women and people of color on board at every level. And finally, Ryan had made many employees wealthy, with generous stock options and giveaways for the most senior employees right down to the most junior. Glamor-a-Go-Go's stock price had grown tenfold during Ryan's tenure—and that was hardly small change.

Beyond his business acumen, Ryan was popular because he was, in a word, charming. He was 50 but had the energy of a man half his age. He also had lost none of the good looks that had made him a bona fide big man on campus back in his days as a football star at Rice University. At Glamor-a-Go-Go, Ryan made it a point to know employees by name, from R&D scientists to factory workers. He spent hours each week bounding around the company's sprawling headquarters with the enthusiasm of a freshly minted entrepreneur, handing out product samples and eagerly soliciting comments. And company lore was replete with stories of Ryan personally helping employees in trouble. When a Glamor-a-Go-Go truck driver found that his young daughter had cancer, Ryan paid for an experimental treatment not covered by insurance. When another employee was in a hospice, Ryan visited him there and presented him with a baseball signed by his favorite Astros player. The door to Ryan's office was almost always open, and it wasn't unusual to see employees stopping in just to share a joke with the CEO, whose laugh was as large as his personality.

Lately, however, a group of senior managers—mainly women—had started to grumble about Ryan's rumored infidelities. When Ryan's secretary, Donna Ulin, quit, after what was thought to be a two-year affair, some questioned her claim about a better job in California. A few members of the board had even wondered if she'd been sexually harassed, fearing that such charges would damage the company—especially since its message was all about Girl Power. Others complained—albeit never to Ryan's face—that Kimberly Crogan, a 24-year-old who started in Glamor-a-Go-Go's mailroom, seemed to move up very quickly after what appeared to be a month-long fling with the CEO. With no manufacturing experience to speak of, Crogan was now a factory supervisor.

"Kimmy Crogan is a smart woman and she'll go far" was Ryan's reply when Roger had asked him about her meteoric rise. "Trust me, I know what I'm doing. Kimmy Crogan will make *great* things happen for us." Such bravado was typical of the CEO. Whenever individual board members questioned his flirtatious behavior in private conversations—it had happened three times, as far as Roger knew—Ryan acted baffled, even offended. He bemoaned the fact that people were misinterpreting simple friendliness. "And I'll remind you," he would say, "no one has ever accused me of anything. No woman has ever come forward and claimed that I've acted inappropriately—because I haven't." That was true. None of Ryan's alleged girlfriends claimed to have had a relationship with him, and some had even publicly denied it.

"I may flirt, but I'm a married man," Ryan once told a board member who queried him about the rumors. "So let's stop gossiping and get back to work."

In the past, such appeals had done the trick. But, Roger wondered, would Joe Ryan be able to talk his way out of this latest scandal?

Roger picked up the phone with a heavy sigh; the voice at the other end was bright and acerbic. "Roger, did you see the fabulous picture in the paper this morning?" Carol Tomkins asked.

"You know what he's going to do, don't you?" Roger replied. "He's going to claim that he and Laura are just friends. Same old story." As he spoke, Roger opened the newspaper again and glanced at the photo. Ryan's arm rested on Laura's shoulder, and they were smiling at each other in a manner that definitely did not look platonic. "Poor Michelle," Roger groaned, thinking of Ryan's wife, a soft-spoken mother of three girls, ages eight to 15.

"Frankly, I'm not worried about Michelle at this point," Carol said. "She's known about Joe for years— she's *had* to. She's obviously decided to stay married to him anyway. I'm worried about Glamor-a-Go-Go. I think Joe's behavior is putting the company at risk."

"Why? Because you're afraid one of his old girl-friends is going to turn up and charge him with sexual harassment?" Roger grimaced, picturing the headlines, which were sure to poke fun at Glamor-a-Go-Go's advertising slogan: "Go All the Way with Glamor-a-Go-Go!"

"A sexual harassment charge is possible," Carol said. "And so is widespread ridicule. I mean, our brand identity could be completely ruined. Think about it, Roger. Think about our Web site—it has all that advice about Girl Power. You know, 'Don't let anyone pressure you into a physical relationship,' and 'Older guys who go after younger girls are creeps,' and on and on . . .

"But even more important," she continued, "I'm worried about the whole question of leadership—of integrity. Can we really expect Glamor-a-Go-Go's employees to pour their hearts and souls into a company that's run by a guy who lies and cheats on his wife? Come on."

Sexual harassment and threats to brand identity concerned him, but Roger wasn't sure about Carol's last point. "Didn't the Monica Lewinsky scandal just prove that Americans don't care about the private lives of their leaders?" Roger asked. "After all, everyone knew Bill Clinton cheated on his wife, but his approval ratings stayed sky high. Everyone has known for years about Joe's philandering, and most people still think he's a great CEO. I'll remind you, Joe claims that he's never cheated on Michelle. And there is no proof that he has."

It was Carol's turn to sigh. "That's right," she said, "and I'm afraid I'll have to hear that lame story all over again this afternoon. Our quarterly board meeting just happens to be at two o'clock. Joe's private life wasn't on the agenda—but it will be now."

The meeting was chaired by Sam Martell, who had been on the Glamor-a-Go-Go board for nearly a decade. A sardonic New Yorker, Martell was a partner at the venture capital firm that had hired Ryan and funded the company's turnaround. Its IPO had made him very rich, and he was, not surprisingly, usually very supportive of the CEO. But Martell also remained a large shareholder. He liked Joe Ryan, but he cared more about Glamor-a-Go-Go.

Martell called the meeting to order by crumpling its agenda into a ball. The other nine members of the board laughed, but not happily. "I trust all of you have seen this morning's local paper," Martell began. "If not, here it is." He held up the picture and read the caption. "I asked Joe to give us some time in an executive session before he joins us."

"I'll vent first," Carol broke in. "Sam, we have a real problem on our hands. People in this room have talked to Joe at least three times about how flagrant his behavior is. And each time, he completely denies any impropriety; he sweet-talks us into focusing on his performance as a CEO. Every time, we do just what he asks. But we'd be irresponsible if we didn't face the fact that his affairs open Glamor-a-Go-Go up to lawsuits and public embarrassment. Just think about that reference to Families First in the newspaper today and our major focus on Girl Power. We could become a laughingstock."

"Not to mention the fact that this is sure to damage morale within the company," added Tim Wheeler, a board member with 40 years of experience in the industry. "No one likes to work for someone they can't respect. I mean—"

Martell held up his hand to stop Wheeler. "Now, wait a minute," he said firmly, "I respect Joe Ryan. I think everyone at this table respects him as a businessman. He has made this company into what it is today—a great place to work with terrific products, first-class manufacturing processes, and a smart strategy for both the short and long terms. In fact, I just got our latest numbers this morning, and they're even better than expected. I have to say—I *respect* Joe Ryan as a CEO.

"And let's remember, shall we, that our first job as members of the board is to represent Glamor-a-Go-Go's shareholders," Martell went on. "Do you really think they care that Joe Ryan had his picture in a little Texas newspaper with some young woman who happens not to be his wife?"

"Absolutely not." It was Mary Lamott speaking, the longest-serving member of the board. Her father had founded the company and served as its CEO for 30 years. Lamott herself had worked behind the counter in Glamor-a-Go-Go's original store. "Think what you want of me," Lamott went on, "but I don't give a hoot who Joe Ryan sleeps with. The nature of his marriage is utterly irrelevant to the shareholders of this company. In fact, I think most of them would have our heads if we fired a top-notch CEO just as the company goes global. And honestly, I don't think Joe's extracurricular behavior matters one whit to the employees either. This is 1999, for God's sake. The president and a 21-year-old intern had sex in the White House—"

"This isn't about sex!" Carol Tomkins cut in. "It's about character."

Carol's statement hung in the air as Sam Martell walked to the door of the boardroom and ushered in Joe Ryan.

What, If Anything, Should Glamor-a-Go-Go's Board Do about Joe Ryan?

Six correspondents offer their advice.

➤ Freada Kapor Klein and Mitchell Kapor

Freada Kapor Klein is a principal of Klein Associates, a firm based in Cambridge, Massachusetts, that surveys, trains, and consults on issues of workplace environment. Mitchell Kapor is a general partner at Accel Partners, a venture capital firm based in Palo Alto, California. He is the founder and former CEO of Lotus Development Corporation and serves on several boards of directors. They occasionally consult together to CEOs and boards of directors. They were recently married.

Glamor-a-Go-Go's board should reframe their discussion. This isn't only about Joe Ryan's sex life or character; just as important is the question of whether the board has been doing its job appropriately. Its members are now operating at a substantial disadvantage: they need to react quickly, but they're not adequately prepared, nor do they have reliable data.

The board is currently polarized—some members see the sexual escapades of the CEO as a business issue, and some think they are irrelevant. Both sides are making arguments about the impact of the CEO's behavior on customer confidence, employee morale, legal liability, and shareholder interests. The trouble is that the board members haven't developed a shared framework that would help them think about these issues. As a result, their course of action will be dictated by the member who is the most articulate or the most powerful.

Undoubtedly, someone will ask the general counsel for an opinion on what course of action would pose the least risk of lawsuits. Given the legal climate in this country, somebody is going to threaten a lawsuit no matter what the board does. Trying to avoid that at all costs would be myopic; instead, the board should figure out what the right thing to do is—and then do it.

If the whole story about Ryan emerges, the board needs to be able to justify its actions to all the company's constituencies: the teenage girls who spend their allowances on Glamor-a-Go-Go's products, the employees who want to be proud of their workplace, and the shareholders who want steady returns and no surprises. How will the board respond when the following information surfaces?

- Ryan's "flirtatious behavior" had come up at least three times in private conversations with members of the board.

- A group of senior managers had expressed concerns about Ryan's behavior.

- Specific employees were widely rumored to have had affairs with Ryan.

- It's very possible that Ryan has lied to—or intentionally misled—board members.

Glamor-a-Go-Go's board should do two things: give Ryan a strict warning and begin to develop a shared framework that will allow it to act responsibly.

First, the warning. Ryan's behavior has a substantial impact on the business's performance—that's a reality. Once pictures start appearing in newspapers, privacy is no longer an issue. The board members should tell Ryan three things: they're going to invite employees to go directly to them with complaints or concerns; he will be terminated if his actions cause a real or perceived conflict of interest; and he will be terminated immediately if they discover that he has lied to them.

Ryan should also be offered help in the form of executive coaching. He must come to understand how employees and customers view his actions and why he continues to engage in self-destructive behaviors. The terms of the coaching relationship should be carefully constructed so that everyone is very clear about who the client is: Ryan or the board of directors.

While admonishment is messy, termination at this point would be unfair. The members of the board had plenty of warning signs; all they did in response was engage in half-hearted conversations. They never gave Ryan a clear message. To fire him under those circumstances would be irresponsible.

Next they need to tackle the issue of how to go forward. Their current discussion would be dramatically different if in the past they had resolved some important questions. Do the board members subscribe to a set of values about who they are and what they believe in? Are their strategy decisions driven by principles or by opportunistic thinking? Do they really believe in the company's "Girl Power" slogan, or is that just a marketing ploy?

Glamor-a-Go-Go should have a set of business principles in place that are more than platitudes. For example, it needs a policy not only on sexual harassment but also on consensual behavior. At a minimum, it should require the disclosure of any consensual relationship that might lead to a conflict of interest. The relationship itself wouldn't be grounds for termination, but nondisclosure of the potential conflict would be.

Glamor-a-Go-Go employees who want to raise questions about sexual harassment, discrimination, office romance, or conflicts of interest should have a direct channel to the board when they feel they can't talk to human resources or to their managers. In addition, all employees, including the CEO, should receive training on how to handle these issues, and the board should hold focused discussions on them.

The board should also collect data through employee and customer surveys. Such data would help resolve speculation over how much Ryan's behavior has damaged employees' confidence in management. It would also indicate what customers expect from the leaders of a company trying to distinguish itself through a values-based campaign.

The board is between a rock and a hard place, but it is partly responsible for putting itself there. As long as sexual behavior in the workplace is approached from only a narrow perspective—fear of lawsuits or concern about individuals' privacy—companies will make mistakes. The continuum from welcome to unwelcome sexual attention in the workplace should be viewed like any other business issue—one that requires thinking in advance and reliance on data and analysis to make the best decisions. There are more than enough unavoidable crises in contemporary business—the sexual behavior of the CEO need not be one of them.

➤ Burke Stinson

Burke Stinson is public relations director at AT&T in Basking Ridge, New Jersey.

Let's face it: getting away with breaking the rules is fun for many inventive, adventurous, and accomplished people. It makes them feel important and larger than life. Legends are made of this behavior—especially in business, sports, and the military, where victory is the primary goal.

But not all legends are good ones, as any public figure suddenly caught up in a scandal can attest. First off, rule-breaking leadership often creates tension and jealousy. People who are less talented and more timid frequently resent it when their high-flying leaders flaunt the rules—all the while feeling envious of the chief's success.

In this particular case, a charismatic CEO is clashing with people who want the rules to be followed. And they do have a point: the public embarrassment of Ryan could affect consumers' perception of the company's products—as well as employees' perceptions of what's considered acceptable behavior at Glamor-a-Go-Go.

Ryan seems like the type of person who would take any discussion about the photo in the morning paper lightly. He's probably faced similar predicaments throughout his career and would have little trouble making a case that no immediate harm to the company or employee morale would result from the incident. Yet in these days of on-line gossip, it is difficult to shrug off nasty news.

Glamor-a-Go-Go's board has to bear in mind Ryan's psychological makeup, the company's personnel guidelines, and the impact of his leadership on both the company and the marketplace. I would suggest that Tim Wheeler and Carol Tomkins prepare a report—perhaps in the form of a damaging newspaper exposé about Ryan, one that hasn't broken yet but could if an enterprising reporter started digging. The story would include excerpts from the company's sexual harassment policy, an example about an employee the company had reprimanded in the past, and a fabricated quotation or two from people who buy Glamor-a-Go-Go products.

Wheeler and Tomkins should give the report to Sam Martell, Ryan's supporter. They must convince him that Ryan's behavior has to change, using the news story to show what would happen if fiction became fact. They need to keep their feelings in check; hand-wringing and scolding won't have any effect on Martell—or anyone else. Martell needs to see that rumors (and facts) about alleged philandering and abuse of power can impact the bottom line.

Finally, Martell must have a one-on-one, no-nonsense talk with Ryan—particularly while the CEO's behavior can still be corrected from the company's viewpoint and the news coverage is confined to a local daily. Martell's advice? "Like Caesar's wife, you must be above reproach. We need you to behave yourself and keep up appearances—whether at grand openings or around the office. Too much is riding on you."

➤ Patrick Carnes

Patrick Carnes is clinical director for sexual disorder services at the Meadows, a facility in Wickenburg, Arizona, that treats people who have addictive and psychiatric disorders.

Ryan's story is commonly heard in clinics that treat sexual disorders and addictions. And corporate officers frequently react the way they did in this case. Let's look at the two main claims, first from Ryan's foes and then from his defenders.

"It's about character." Sexual behavior usually is about character. The choices one makes reflect one's sense of responsibility and judgment. But for some people, sexual behavior is an addictive illness. Just as some people gamble, eat, or use drugs and alcohol compulsively, so too do some use sex repetitively and self-destructively. They don't understand some of the things they do, nor do they even want to do them. On the inside, they feel nothing but shame and despair. On the outside, they usually deny that they have a problem and expend a great deal of effort convincing others of the truth of that claim.

There is not enough information in the case to determine if Ryan is a sex addict. But let's assume he is. If that were true, his affairs would be the tip of the iceberg. More than likely, he would also be engaging in other sexual behaviors, such as compulsive visits to prostitutes and frequent cybersex. His parents or other relatives probably have problems with addiction. And, as is usually the case with sex addicts, he would likely have been a victim of childhood sexual, physical, and emotional abuse. Addicts often compulsively repeat the scenarios of their abuse.

Apart from his apparent sexual compulsion, Ryan appears to be conscientious and ethical. That means we can probably rule out sociopathy or extreme narcissism as a diagnosis. There's no evidence of alcohol or drug abuse, which would be typical, but he does engage in some high-risk behaviors, which is also typical. The picture in the paper makes that clear. Again, assuming that he is a sex addict, he needs help. Treatment can restore a valued employee and reduce the risk and performance problems that generally stem from sex addiction. That brings us to the second perceptual problem.

"It won't affect the company." Roger Cushing argues that the Clinton outcome shows leadership is not affected by sex scandals. But the President and the country did suffer consequences. And it's well established that there is always a negative impact on productivity and corporate culture in these cases. In the past, Ryan has assured the board that no complaints will be lodged. As a sex addict, he would have confidence that a combination of manipulation, charm, or depth of relationship would protect him from litigation. The CEOs, physicians, and clergy we treat always believe that no legal action will result from their behavior—but they are nearly always wrong.

So what should the board do? The problem it has now is a lack of data. One thing it can do is conduct a "harassment audit." It is a common risk management practice to have an outside investigator talk with current and former employees. Sometimes the results are astounding. I recently worked with a company in which two complaints had been filed against the CEO, who described them as "baseless." An outside investigator conducted an audit. Close to 100 women employees spoke of affairs, propositions, or fondling. An expanded investigation revealed that the man had approached vendors, neighbors, family friends, and even his daughter-in-law. These women did not come forward for many of the same reasons that women may have protected Ryan. He was known to be likable, kind, and talented. And everyone he worked with benefited from his competence.

If data show that there's a serious problem, trusted supervisors or colleagues can have a frank talk with Ryan. Sometimes that's all that's needed. If addiction is the problem, addicts usually know they are in trouble; sometimes they welcome help. Sometimes an intervention by a therapist familiar with the corporate world is in order. For an intervention to work, all the participants need to be familiar with basic concepts about sex addiction—just as they would with alcoholism or compulsive gambling.

When an employee is in trouble with sex, the easiest response is either to ignore the problem or to fire the person.

But corporations frequently confront the issue when the person is vital to the organization's future. They must get beyond prejudices. If they do, they may find at the bottom of the situation a treatable illness. And when the person is treated, they may gain an even more valuable employee as a result.

➢ Daryl Koehn

Daryl Koehn holds the Cullen Chair in Business Ethics at the University of St. Thomas in Houston.

The members of the board need to confront Ryan about his alleged behavior. They should talk with him about how his own ethics are inextricably tied to his ability to lead the company and perhaps even threaten him with termination if he attempts to stonewall them or evade their queries.

The board members are divided right now because, like most Americans, they're unsure about the relationship between character and ethically acceptable behavior in the workplace. One side maintains that character can't be compartmentalized: someone who exercises poor judgment in one sphere is likely to make bad choices in another. The other side holds that personal ethics are separate from professional ethics. A person can function in a fully professional manner while engaging in off-hours behavior that others might find offensive. Tomkins and Wheeler lean toward the first view. Others—like Martell and Mary Lamott—are committed to the second view. Both views have some merit, and they are not mutually exclusive.

Let's start with the idea that the issue of character can't be divided into personal and professional behavior. The Greek word for character—*ethos*—means acquiring a habit of making choices in a certain way. The idea is that what we do in one area of our lives tends to affect actions in others because we become habituated to telling ourselves that certain behaviors are justified. Those who hold this view believe that it's a serious ethical mistake to draw a hard-and-fast line between our private and our professional lives.

I know of one case in which some bank employees saw a bank manager snorting cocaine at a party. The employees did not report this drug use to the manager's boss. They reasoned that what the manager did on his own time was entirely his own business. But they should have been more concerned: the bank manager was subsequently found guilty of embezzling large sums of money from the company to support his drug addiction.

If we continually rationalize questionable behavior outside the office—"It's okay to take drugs because it's not hurting anyone else"—there is nothing to stop us from explaining away corrupt behavior at work—"It's okay to steal from my employer because the company is not paying me what I'm worth." If Ryan is having affairs with his female subordinates and then lying about it, he may well lie in other circumstances. He may, for example, feel free to misrepresent the company's performance to boost the value of his stock options. Before meeting with Ryan, the board should ask the audit subcommittee to scrutinize the company's "better than expected" numbers.

At the same time, the people defending Ryan are partly right: professional and personal ethics are not always one and the same. Professionals have skills that are task specific. If a doctor can heal us, we aren't likely to pay much attention to rumors about her marriage. As long as people's private lives do not impair their specific competencies, we tend to view their quirks, habits, and tastes as largely irrelevant to our judgment of their performance.

However, the separation of the public and private spheres is never absolute. When task competencies are directly threatened by weaknesses of character—or by a major gap between personal and professional practice—we become alarmed. As information about character comes to light, we reassess people's abilities to carry out their work. What parent, for example, would trust a pediatrician if it became known that he liked to look at child pornography after hours? Who would trust an American Lung Association executive who had major stock holdings in tobacco companies?

The key question, therefore, is whether Ryan's behavior is undermining his task-specific competence: business leadership. The board has warned him at least three times about his behavior, yet Ryan continues to dismiss its concerns. His cavalier refusal to heed his colleagues' advice is a public and professional matter that raises serious doubts about his leadership abilities. Ryan is a golden boy for now, but leaders do not live by charm alone. If Glamor-a-Go-Go falls on hard times or gets slapped with a sexual harassment lawsuit, the company will need a CEO who is willing and able to respond meaningfully to the concerns of fellow managers, board members, employees, shareholders, and community members. Ryan's habitual strategy of denying that a problem exists will be unacceptable under those conditions.

All leaders need the respect of their followers. After all, Ryan did not increase the company's stock price by himself. The increase in Glamor-a-Go-Go's value is largely due to the hard work of employees who believe in the company and in the values Ryan communicates. Because Ryan refuses to change his behavior, his colleagues are questioning whether he deserves their respect. Some suspect that he has been sexually harassing his subordinates. It is only a matter of time before other employees begin to believe that the company has a double standard.

Like many American companies, Glamor-a-Go-Go may have required all employees to sign an ethics code as a condition of employment. These codes typically require employees to avoid even the appearance of a conflict of interest or of improper behavior. If such a code is in place, the CEO shouldn't be allowed to violate ethical rules that all other employees must adhere to. Although some employees may be willing to overlook Ryan's sexual peccadilloes, the majority will not tolerate hypocrisy and favoritism.

The board needs to put these arguments to Ryan. If he denies that a problem exists, the board should be prepared to threaten him with termination. Ryan cannot continue to ignore the impact of his behavior on colleagues, subordinates, and the larger community.

➤ Lisa A. Mainiero

Lisa A. Mainiero is a professor of management at the Fairfield University School of Business in Connecticut and the author of Office Romance *(Rawson, 1989).*

Move over, Bill Clinton. These days, cupid is blowing kisses on company time. The workplace now serves as a dating service for many couples, spawning numerous office affairs. Most companies don't have a big problem with relationships between unmarried peers. But what should a company do when relationships appear improper for one reason or another?

No corporate policy on God's green earth can prevent people from falling in love at the office. But companies should be concerned when employees' love lives create conflicts of interest and raise questions about job performance. Some have policies designed to discipline people whose behavior may hurt the company.

When affairs cross hierarchical lines, the lower-level lover may benefit from undeserved raises, promotions, or even costly business trips. In such cases, the boss is not doing his job, the subordinate may find herself in a position she's not qualified for, and other people's productivity may fall as they see how rewards are doled out. And consider the potential conflicts of interest when employees from different departments have affairs. A relationship between a company accountant and a sales rep who regularly turns in a monthly expense report could be cause for concern.

But in truth, most managers look the other way when they see that an affair is taking place. If job performance suffers, then termination becomes likely; if job performance is fine, the two people may simply get a slap on the wrist and an admonition not to kiss in the hallways. That was the result in Bill Clinton's case, and it is the most likely scenario with Ryan.

Let's look at the facts in this case. First, despite people's suspicions, no one has ever caught Ryan "in the act," so to speak. Second, none of Ryan's alleged paramours have made a claim of sexual harassment. Third, and this is critically important, although one woman has enjoyed rapid promotion, there is no *pattern* of sex being traded for power. Fourth, the women who have supposedly been involved with Ryan have denied any wrongdoing. Fifth, the guy is still—amazingly perhaps—married. Sixth, there's no indication that the job performance of any of the characters has suffered.

Given the evidence—or rather, the lack of evidence—it would be difficult to fire the CEO at this point. The board should have a discussion with Ryan to let him know about the rumors that are circulating and their potential impact on Glamor-a-Go-Go's bottom line. He should be reprimanded and warned to keep his private life strictly private. He also needs to be reminded that as a leader his actions are closely scrutinized. And the way people perceive his actions is extremely important; when perceptions linger long enough, they eventually become as good as facts. My advice to Ryan is this: You should scrawl in permanent marker the saying "Don't fish off the company pier" on your office wall . . . and on your computer screen . . . and on your briefcase . . . and on your tie. Your future with Glamor-a-Go-Go may depend on taking that message to heart.

Originally published in September–October 1999

Reprint 99511

SARAH CLIFFE

What a Star—
What a Jerk

Executive Summary

After a long stint in consulting, Jane Epstein has just become a manager at TechniCo. She's trying to get a fix on the various personalities and roles of her new coworkers, and by and large, she seems to have inherited a pretty good team. One's got a lot of social capital built up; another seems to be a natural salesperson. Something about Andy Zimmerman, though, has her worried.

At first she can't put her finger on it—maybe he's a bit too aggressive? But as time passes, she watches Andy's mean streak show itself again and again: He belittles administrative assistants for minor mistakes, ruthlessly cuts down colleagues when they present

Executive Summary

ideas that aren't fully developed, and makes everyone in the group feel small and stupid. But Andy has another side: He's usually right, and he's very, very good at his job. As another manager tells Jane, "the guy won't win any personality contests, but you'll love his numbers." In fact, in terms of pure performance, he's the best Jane's got. She'd be crazy not to want him in her group.

And yet, she can't deny that Andy's behavior is undermining morale and hurting the team's financial performance. Now Jane's feeling frustrated. When she left her consulting job for this position, she expected to focus on numbers, products, customers—on building something. Instead, she finds that people issues are taking up most of her time.

This fictional case study explores the dynamics that occur when a star performer has a highly abrasive personality. Four commentators advise Jane on how she can curb Andy's bad behavior without hurting the team's bottom line.

From: Jane Epstein
To: Rick Lazarus
Sent: 5/14/01
Subject: settling in

Hi Rick. I'm starting to get settled in at TechniCo—I miss you and the rest of the gang, and the adrenaline of working with clients when I'm *on,* but I'm thrilled not to be living in airports anymore. Hope Mary and the kids are well.

I've inherited a good team here. They're all strong performers, and most of them are nice, too. I'm sure they're still wondering about me—but so far, so good. Partial cast: Caroline's been here longest; she seems pragmatic, very good with people. Juggling work-family issues and a recent divorce—but she pulls her weight and then some. She's universally trusted (I think). Tom's the joker. A natural sales guy—a bouncy golden retriever personality that cloaks real drive, know what I mean? You never really get inside, but there don't seem to be many internal climate changes anyway. Jack's intense, maybe an intellectual—I haven't quite figured him out. I think he may be shy (?). Anyhow, then there's Andy Zimmerman, who's got me slightly worried—maybe because he intimidates me just a bit. He's very bright, but he's aggressive—doesn't suffer fools gladly. He'll bear watching, I think.

Better run. By the way, I love being back in Minneapolis. And, glory be, the hometown team is making us proud.

From: Rick Lazarus
To: Jane Epstein
Sent: 5/14/01
Subject: Hey stranger

Good to hear from you, Jane. The Twins have got people talking, all right. Though of course they'll fold when the Yankees hit their stride. ;)

What's got you nervous about this Zimmerman guy? –R

Sent: 5/15/01
Subject: re: Hey stranger

Nothing I can put my finger on. Here's a little incident. My AA, Maureen, flubbed a meeting time—scheduled over something else—and he really lit into her. Not the end of the world—she had made a mistake, and he had to rearrange an appointment—but he could have gotten the point across more tactfully. And she is *my* AA. (And I am *his* boss, and he did it in front of me.)–Jane

Sent: 5/15/01

Subject: don't be a softie

J – The guy doesn't necessarily sound like a problem to me. I hate it when people screw up scheduling, and you've always been too patient with that kind of thing. Clearly you have to establish your own authority with him, though, or he'll step all over you.

What's the place like in general? Are the folks there patient with incompetence? Or is it crisp and cruel, like here? ;) By the by, Mary sends her love. –R

Sent: 5/16/01

Subject: tougher than you think

Funny you should ask. It's hardly crisp and cruel. In fact, it's probably a little too nicey-nice. Support staff's not up to the same standards (not paid as well, either). And there's a little more coasting among professional staff here. (Culling out the bottom 20% of performers every year sure keeps people on their toes!) Senior managers talk a lot about lack of hierarchy, which seems to translate into tolerating barely average performance if the people are well liked. (Then again, this could be all wrong: I'm describing a place I've only been part of for a few weeks.) –Jane

Sent: 5/22/01

Subject: FW: good for a laugh . . .

You have just received the Amish virus. Since we have no electricity or computers, you are on the honor system. Please delete all of your files on your hard drive. Then forward this message to everyone in your address book.

Thank thee.

Sent: 5/22/01
Subject: ha!

Speaking of honor (not), here's another anecdote in the continuing "Who is Andy Zimmerman" saga. Yesterday we were doing some strategizing as a group. (We need to be more aggressive about growth, and this was a pretty open-ended meeting to think about new markets.) Jack (the intense, possibly shy one that I haven't figured out yet) was going on a bit too long about a pet idea of his. I was about to redirect the conversation when Andy cut him off: "What you're proposing makes no sense, and here's why." Then he laid out all the flaws in poor Jack's thinking, one by one—really made him squirm. The thing is, he was right. On the other hand, it was a preliminary, semibrainstorming kind of meeting, so his tirade stopped the free flow of ideas in its tracks.

Later, I heard him *reaming* out the group's other AA, Danielle: "This is an important customer. He's called three times—WHY CAN'T YOU GET IT RIGHT!?!?" Once again, he was right. But that kind of tongue-lashing *causes* people to make mistakes. –Jane

Sent: 5/22/01
Subject: bottom line?

Ignoring his niceness quotient for a moment, how's the guy's performance? –Rick

Sent: 5/22/01
Subject: re: bottom line?

I don't think he'd have gotten away with his nastiness for so long if his performance weren't topflight. As another group leader said to me over coffee, "The guy won't win any personality contests, but you'll love his numbers." He brings home the bacon: He's smart, efficient—the best we've got (in terms of pure performance). I'd have to be crazy not to want him in my group. –J

Sent: 5/22/01
Subject: re: re: bottom line?

Well, then, I don't see the problem. I think you're overreacting. –R

Sent: 5/23/01
Subject: re: re: re: bottom line?

That's what I like about you, Rick—never one to sugarcoat . . .

Sent: 5/30/01
Subject: Holy jelly, Batman . . . we're in a jam!

Can I bore you again with Andy, my low-likability, high-performance guy? Until now, I'd thought he was just nasty to lower-level people (which I quietly asked him to tone down, btw, after the incidents with the AAs) but at least grudgingly civil to colleagues. But he's gone and alienated Caroline, the one who's going through the divorce. Background: She has huge social capital built up here; she's the one everyone turns to with their problems, either professional or personal. She's a good egg, but she isn't at her best right now (a custody issue got messy and her mother's sick). She probably should have taken some time off, but it's a bad time of year—so I asked her to hold off. Okay, so here she is, this normally centered person who's hanging on by a thread, and Andy got under her skin. She forwarded me this e-mail he'd sent her, and when I went to talk to her about it, she cried. It was a *horrible* scene. Anyhow, take a look: "Caroline, you screwed up big time. We had a meeting with people I'd been trying to cultivate for eight months, set up well in advance, and you blew it off at the last minute, which embarrassed me and endangered the business. I can just hear you whining, 'Things are a mess at home right now'—but you know what? Tough. Everybody's got problems, and they should stay out of the office. If I don't land this business, it will be because of your incompetence, and you can bet that Epstein and everyone else who counts will hear about it."

After she was done crying—which embarrassed us both a lot—she expressed remorse for making the mistake. Then we talked . . . she explained how she has sort of "handled" Zimmerman until recently (which is why she felt betrayed by his accusations). Evidently, he'd often vent to her about what he saw as all-around stupidity. She'd listen, calm him down, and occasionally chide him extremely gently for being out of line. And other people would come to her and complain when he'd said something nasty, and she'd calm *them* down (explaining the pressure he was under, whatever). Since he exempted her from his nastiness, she was shocked when he turned on her. Anyhow, she wasn't trying to blow the whistle on him—not really— but I could see that she was fed up with the smoothing-over role. (I gather that my predecessor completely ignored the whole situation—in part because Caroline kept it under control. Sure wish I could do that.)

Obviously, I have to have a chat with the big bad wolf. You know, when I left BCP to take a job with a real company, I imagined focusing on numbers, products, customers—on *building* something. Instead, I feel as if people issues—stupid little blowups like this— take up most of my time. Sheesh. These are all highly paid people, mostly with advanced degrees. . . . Why do I feel like a kindergarten teacher?

Sent: 5/30/01
Subject: could be worse . . .

J—In some ways, he sounds like your bad cop: He keeps laggards in line, you get to be the nice guy. I could imagine worse set-ups.

I'm surprised she showed you that memo, since it makes her look bad. I know you're going to tell me it's abusive, but is it, really?

Sent: 5/30/01

Subject: re: could be worse . . .

Abusive? I don't know. But it is threatening. And it makes someone who's good, and who's defended him in the past, feel like garbage. . . . Oh, I don't know what I think.—J

Sent: 5/31/01

Subject: whew

Okay, so Andy and I had a long talk. I think it went reasonably well. With Caroline's permission, I told him about the leave she should be on. And he said he had to admit that he'd never seen anything like that from her before. Looked very slightly ashamed (but maybe I imagined that part).

I wanted to establish some kind of rapport, as well as call him on inappropriate behavior, so I got him talking about his own role in the group and how he sees the work developing over the next several months. And—surprise, surprise—we had a good conversation. He's got great insights, energy, and smarts. We talked for quite some time, in a way that was, to be honest, more productive and visionary and (simultaneously) down-to-earth than would have happened had the whole group been present. We were sort of firing off each other in the same way you and I used to—it was fun. :)

Of course, I went back to the question of how he acts in the group. I said, basically, "Look, you're talented and quick and impatient, and you just have to slow down and bite your tongue and be a little nicer to people." (Since we'd been having a really good conversation—with the temporary intimacy that creates—it was easy to say.) He was somewhat dismissive but, when I pushed it, he agreed to try to listen better in meetings and stop reaming out the AAs.

Sent: 5/31/01
Subject: words to live by . . .
I always said you'd make a great kindergarten teacher <ducks>. So problem boy is tamed?

If perchance he isn't, just remember what Groucho Marx said: "Time wounds all heels." –R

Sent: 6/01/01
Subject: re: words to live by . . .
Groucho didn't say that, Jane Sherwood Ace did. :) And yes, let's decide problem boy is tamed, and forget about it. –Jane

Sent: 6/12/01
Subject: too good to be true
Hey Rick, how was Hawaii? Bet the kids loved the beach—I'm jealous. I could use a little time off myself.

Of course it was too good to be true—problem boy being reformed (sigh). Yesterday I came into a meeting I'd asked him to chair until I could get there. I slipped in quietly—not wanting to disturb things—and the way the room was set up, he didn't see me at first. Every person in that room looked cowed: eyes down, hunched over—slightly squelched in this rather sad way. And it's a good group, really! He was responding to something Tom had said, and his ugly side was out in full force. He sneered, used dismissive language— even rolled his eyes when Tom tried to break in with a counterargument. And this was *after* I'd slipped into his range of vision—who knows what terrors he was up to before I got there? It suddenly became clear to me: This guy's a bully.

Afterwards, I saw Caroline and Tom talking—about Andy, I'm sure. Meanwhile, when I walked into Andy's office a few minutes after the meeting—and looked at him, stone cold—he just shrugged and shook his head.

Damn. He ain't changin'. And this isn't kinder-garten—it's a business. I feel like I'm between a rock (the lousy effect he has on the group) and a hard place (his stellar performance).

What Should Jane Do About Her Top Performer's Mean Streak?

Four commentators offer their advice.

➤ Mary Rowe

Mary Rowe teaches negotiations and conflict management at the Sloan School of Management at MIT in Cambridge, Massachusetts, and is an MIT ombudsperson.

I'm going to approach this problem as if I were TechniCo's organizational ombudsperson—which means that I'm a confidential neutral. I'm an informal coach and shuttle diplomat within the company, looking into problems and working toward systemic changes.

Jane should prepare for this challenge as she would for a project launch. She needs to quickly collect a lot of information. And she must protect everyone's privacy—including Andy's—along the way.

She should start by gathering information about the people involved and the context of the organizational setting. Does the company have policies about mean behavior—perhaps a "core values" statement about "dignity and respect at TechniCo"? Official statements like this—and good training programs—can offer managers much-needed help and support. Other questions to ask: Would her bosses want to know about the problems with Andy? Is he following the tone set by TechniCo's top executives, or would they want to see Andy's behavior change? Is there a person from HR who could be helpful? And how is the company doing? What are Jane's team's interests? What are the technical and interpersonal skills of the other team members?

Next, Jane should analyze her own interests and power, as well as Andy's. Does she have strong power to reward and sanction? Does she have moral authority, derived from company policy or her own character? What's her technical expertise? Does she have a fallback position if this situation goes bad? As for Andy's interests and sources of power: Does he want a new assignment? Is he indispensable? Does he have other offers? Finally, she should consider the various kinds of power each team member wields: Do any of them have other offers? Might a desperate Caroline complain about Andy to her old friend the CEO?

If, after analyzing the situation and considering the interests and power of all parties, Jane decides to work directly with Andy, she'll need to get his attention. She might suggest that he watch the movie *What Women Want* or that he take the quiz in Harry Levinson's 1978 HBR article, "The Abrasive Personality." Alternatively, a tough order from Jane's boss, transmitted through her, might capture Andy's attention, if that option is appropriate. Notice that I didn't suggest that she directly confront him. She should ask him to work *with* her to develop an elegant solution—one that satisfies all the interests at stake.

In general, the worst thing a supervisor can do is to sometimes reward and sometimes punish unacceptable behavior. This is even worse than simply rewarding harsh behavior, since the cycle of reward and punishment may make a person immune to rebuke, counseling, and discipline. Ignoring unacceptable behavior is only marginally better than rewarding it, but neither method changes behavior. Jane may punish Andy, but it probably won't change him. Rewarding Andy for excellent behavior may be more effective, especially if the specific behavior of Andy that is rewarded blocks the behavior Jane wants to change.

For example, Andy might be rewarded for mentoring that results in sensational performance by coworkers. In parallel, Andy might be shown that his mean behavior doesn't improve the performance of teammates—that he should affirm their good performance, instead. The best solution will be one that Andy helps to design, so long as it's fair to the rest of the team, even if it is just that Andy becomes an individual contributor.

Whatever happens, Jane needs to keep careful records and follow up. If it turns out that Andy should be fired, she needs backup plans. On the other hand, if Andy succeeds wonderfully, she should think about ways to reward his turnaround.

➤ Chuck McKenzie

Chuck McKenzie is a senior vice president and managing director at Oppenheimer Funds. He is based in New York.

I know Andy pretty well. Everywhere I've worked, we've always had Andys. And we survived them. In some ways, we thrived because of them. But you can't just let the Andys of this world run wild—adjustments on all sides have to be made.

Jane's facing a classic situation: the rainmaker who drives everyone around him crazy. She can't get rid of him, but she can't let him destroy the team, either. The group's morale and its business performance are inextricably entwined. If Andy seriously damages morale—and productivity along with it—he will damage the bottom line. There's even a business case to be made against Andy: It can cost up to ten times as much to bring in new business as it does to hold onto existing business. So no matter how big a rainmaker Andy is, if his actions endanger existing business—perhaps because turnover rates start to skyrocket—that's a serious, bottom-line problem.

But it would probably be foolish to fire Andy. He generates more revenue than anyone else, he has great ideas, and he's extremely smart. In my experience, many outstanding performers are difficult and abrasive. If Jane and her group can cope with true diversity—the diversity that comes with clashing personalities—they'll be a stronger and more creative group.

Jane also needs to define success for her group. If her definition optimizes a range of measures—including new sales, existing-business retention, employee retention, morale, and productivity—she should be able to get everyone rowing in the same direction.

Once Jane has thought through these issues, she needs to make changes in four areas.

Organizational Structure. If the Andys I've worked with are any indication, this Andy isn't going to change much. (I had to laugh when Jane thought one extremely indirect conversation was going to change this guy.) Rather than wasting time on that hopeless strategy, carve out a role that lets him focus on what he's best at: developing sales plans and selling. Give him his own AA (he is the rainmaker, after all) and let them work as a sales team. Meet with Andy regularly one on one, and separate him from the rest of the group as much as possible. That may require redrawing the org chart.

Attitude. Jane needs to adjust her own attitude. She wants to be a leader—somebody above the fray who sets direction and thinks about strategy—not a manager. But in this case, she's going to have to address the messy, everyday stuff before she gets a chance to lead.

Roles. The roles in Jane's group are poorly defined: Caroline is playing full-time counselor to the group, and Andy is micromanaging everyone and everything. The team members are bound to be confused as a result, and productivity is sure to go down. Jane needs to clarify each person's responsibilities. (If she starts to fulfill her own responsibilities, and clearly defines Andy's, the rest may take care of itself.)

Culture. Jane has noted that TechniCo is too tolerant of barely average performers. If she can change that cultural norm within her own group, she'll improve the group's performance and productivity, as well as her own career prospects. It would probably appeal to Andy, too. (I'm not deluding myself—people like Andy always think that they're better than everyone else. But at least he'd have fewer legitimate reasons for his blowups.)

Managing an Andy isn't easy. Some managers think people like him should be nurtured, promoted, and fawned over.

Doing that creates too many problems for the rest of the organization, in my opinion. But it's also not possible to take the high road and say, "We won't tolerate unpleasant behavior." In the real world, managers need to carve out places for unpleasant, highly productive people—places that keep them from poisoning everyone else's working environment. It isn't easy, but it can be done.

➤ Kathy Jordan

Kathy Jordan, a psychologist, is an executive coach with KRW International, a global executive-development consulting firm. She is based in Boston.

Jane's biggest problem right now isn't actually Andy Zimmerman. It's learning to be a manager. Jane seems to think that people issues are distracting her from her "real" job. ("I imagined focusing on numbers, products, customers . . . instead, I feel as if . . . stupid little blowups . . . take up most of my time.") She needs to realize that managing people is her real job.

It's fine to watch a new group for a while, analyzing behavior patterns before jumping to action. Nevertheless, Jane seems too passive. She is spending too much time observing garden-variety interpersonal dynamics that demand a response. When Andy eviscerated Jack's ideas during an early meeting, for example, Jane should have interrupted, reminded the team that they were in brainstorming mode, and suggested getting everyone's ideas on the table before evaluating anything in detail. She needs to give Andy more than "stone cold" looks when he has been rude and dismissive.

As a manager, Jane's most pressing task is to develop a high-performing team. Luckily, she has inherited a reasonably strong group with a typical cast of characters, representing no unusual managerial challenges. Even Andy, her problem employee, is a common type who has held the team, and perhaps TechniCo, hostage to his bad behavior because he delivers the numbers.

First, Jane must be clear with Andy about her expectations. He needs to understand that good numbers are not enough and that his job depends on his ability to manage relationships with colleagues professionally. Instead of allowing herself to be seduced by Andy's insight, Jane needs to bite the bullet and insist on positive behavior as a condition of employment. A potential obstacle might be TechniCo's cultural willingness to accept bad behavior in service to the bottom line. Jane will need to influence opinion leaders by making the case that more collaborative and collegial behavior will improve the financial performance of the team as a whole.

Second, Jane should coach her team members on developing assertiveness and conflict management strategies. Since some of Andy's negative behavior happens in meetings, the entire team would probably benefit from training in how to conduct effective meetings. Andy is currently incapable of chairing a productive meeting, and the rest of the team has no idea how to get a meeting back on track after Andy has derailed it. Creating a team that's able to handle its own work relationships would allow Jane to avoid the trap of becoming a "kindergarten teacher," a trap that's inevitable if she replaces Caroline as Andy's handler.

Finally, Jane has to stop sending e-mail to Rick Lazarus. Because they worked together recently in the same company, he's probably just reinforcing her managerial blind spots. She should find a trustworthy coach who is a seasoned manager at TechniCo. A good internal coach can help in several ways. He or she can give Jane a crash course on corporate culture and help her figure out what kind of leverage she has with Andy. A coach can also help Jane identify who needs to be consulted, or at least kept in the loop, about how she is managing Andy. (A rainmaker like Andy probably has the protection of important senior managers, whose support she will need if she is to influence Andy or, if necessary, to clear the way for his departure.) A coach would also let Jane vet her ideas for deploying staff and managing the business. A good coach might have questioned the wisdom of asking Caroline to defer a much-needed personal leave, for example.

Honeymoons are stunningly short in today's corporate environments, and Jane has only a few months to demonstrate that she understands TechniCo's culture well enough to lead her team into the future. If she takes action now, she might be able to prove her mettle.

➤ James Waldroop

James Waldroop, a psychologist, is a principal at Peregrine Partners, a consulting firm in Brookline, Massachusetts, that specializes in executive development and employee retention.

One of the best managers I ever worked with had what he called a "no creeps" hiring policy. "I don't care how much money somebody could make us, or how smart they are; it's not worth it if they disrupt the entire group," he'd say. Jane may eventually come to see the wisdom of that policy. But let's assume for the time being that she wants to hold on to Andy.

Andy is extremely narcissistic: It's all about *him*—whether he looks good, no matter what. (Even when Caroline is on the ropes, he'll let her have it if she makes him look bad.) His narcissism has another component: It's all about him, *now*. He doesn't take the time to think about how his actions at this moment are going to affect even his own ability to perform over the long term, never mind how they affect other people.

Andy's colleagues have been accommodating his behavior for so long that he has come to see it as all right. When an exasperated Jane compared her job to that of a kindergarten teacher, she wasn't far off. Kids need—and want—limits. Some adults need them, too, and Andy is one of those adults. It's time for Jane to stop accommodating Andy (or "enabling" him, as the drug treatment folks would say) and start setting clear limits.

As his manager, I would alternately stroke his ego ("You're so bright and you really know your stuff") and hammer him hard—hard enough to really rattle him ("But you know, Andy, if you were dying of thirst, I doubt that anyone you work with would toss you a bottle of water"). I'd appeal to his grandiosity ("If you could learn to control your temper and your ego, you could be great, really great . . .") and at the same time, I would raise his anxiety and insecurity levels (". . . but I'm afraid we're wasting our time talking about this, because you don't seem to want to change"). And when I say "alternately," I don't mean from one meeting to the next, I mean from one *minute* to the next. To get through Andy's defenses, Jane will have to jam his radar and scramble his internal radio signals.

"I'd love to keep you here, Andy, but you're one expensive piece of equipment—you cause a lot of damage as you do your job. And the bottom line is [here comes the limit setting—delivered with a steely gaze, if possible] your behavior is totally unprofessional. I know that you mean to do your best for the organization [letting him save a little face here], but you're not even doing that. Being 'right' and being 'effective' aren't even close to synonymous. And although you may be right a lot of the time, you're not nearly as effective as you could be." All this is to set him up for the real choice:

"So, Andy, you need to decide very soon whether you want to work here. Your behavior is out of bounds, and I won't have it. If you decide you want to stay, I'll support you, and I'll do my best to help you to rein in your outbursts. I'd love to see you learn to be more effective. But, to be very clear [steely gaze again], if you fall back into bullying people, I'll initiate action to get you out of here. So go mull this over, and let's talk again."

Now that I've stirred him up, I want him to have to sit with it, so I'd try to have this meeting on a Friday afternoon and arrange the second talk for Monday. That way, he'll be forced to think about it all weekend.

With Andy, Jane has to put a dramatic end to business as usual. She has to hit him hard enough to really get him to listen, she has to set firm limits, and she has to stroke his underlying insecurity enough that he doesn't just walk away. Will it work? I don't know, but it's the best shot she's got.

Originally published in September 2001

Reprint R0108A

When Your Star Performer Can't Manage

Executive Summary

Vic, the CEO of a sporting goods company in this fictional case study, is pleased with the numbers. For several years now, they've gone steadily in one direction: up. But there's trouble in paradise. Hidden from the public's view of industry-dominating winners—from the coolest snowboards to the hottest in-line skates—lies a product development department that my be ready to shatter like cheap fiberglass.

There's one reason in particular for the dark rumblings that periodically reach Vic, and his name is Linus Carver. Carver, the company's chief of product development, is the workaholic mad genius who is responsible for most—he might say all—of the company's successful products. At the same time, he has managed to alienate the rest of his staff, including the two whizkid Generation Xers he brought in. He has been charged with everything from stealing ideas to squashing the initiative of the rest of the team.

From his perch as CEO, Vic preaches "team." And he's even made a few stabs at reining Carver in—his latest move has been to recommend that his mercurial star get some coaching. But Vic also knows who butters his bread. In short, he's bewildered.

Four commentators suggest how Vic can keep the company's product-development group intact and its sales growth strong.

The day began well enough. I got to the office at about 8 A.M., grabbed a cup of coffee, and sat down to the latest issue of the *Rosensteiner Investinfo Report* on Nuf Fun, the sporting goods company where I'm CEO. It always gives me a kick to read the analysts' reports, and this one was no exception. First the Company Description: "Denver-based Nuf Fun is a widely diversified manufacturer of branded leisure products catering to active sporting/recreational participation, including Alpine and cross-country skiing, climbing, parasailing, and various water sports." Then the Investment Conclusion, which was real favorable. A sharp knock on my office door interrupted my reading, and the assistant director of the product development team, Verity Hinde, came in.

"Morning, Verity," I said. "Did you know that since 1991, our sales have advanced at a compounded growth rate of 17%? Net sales have moved up from $218.7 million in 1993 to $367.9 million by second quarter 1996."

"Reading *Rosensteiner* again?" she said in a cool way. "With you, Vic, if it isn't strategy, it's figures. And now you're going to tell me that earnings have gone up at a compounded rate of 24%. With any luck, you'll give me your diversity speech, too." She raised her chin at me and laughed. "How does it go?" She sat down in one of the armchairs across from my desk and waved her arm at my collection of miniature Nuf Fun products in the glass case on the wall. "One of Nuf Fun's real big advantages is its diversity—no one single product category accounts for more than 15% of overall sales." Pointing at each item, she went on: "Skis, snowboards, in-line skates, tents, backpacks, parachutes, delta gliders, and soon, fishing gear."

"I don't have a model of the new ski yet. But the launch is set for the last week in October."

"Vic," she said. "I didn't come here to talk about sales or our highly fragmented market or the new ski. I came to talk about Carver. Again."

I rubbed my eyes. Linus Carver is the head of the product development group. Engineering, design, they all report to him. I thought I knew what Hinde was going to say, so I said, "Whatever it is, shouldn't you take it up with Carver first?"

Hinde opened the writing case she had brought with her and fished out a fountain pen and a yellow legal pad littered with notes. "I've tried. Yesterday I told him morale was sinking, and he just shrugged it off."

"Morale always sinks right after product trials. It's the slump before the next big push."

"He said I was seeing ghosts."

"Maybe you are."

"I figured you'd say that, Vic." She raised herself off the chair and walked over to the window behind me, where she started tapping her pen on the glass. "I'm not seeing ghosts, I'm seeing a product development team in trouble."

"We've come up with two new product lines this year."

She moved to where I could see her. "We haven't come up with two new lines, Carver has."

"Then how do you explain the fact that there are more than 275 ideas in the new-product-idea file?"

She came back around the desk and sat down again. "All I know is, none of the designers feel that they can go to Carver with an idea—because when someone does, he immediately says to fill out all the forms in the procedure manual—"

I cut her off. "You and everybody else in product development approved that policy."

"You didn't let me finish. While you're filling out the forms, he's rushing ahead and putting together a preliminary assessment of his own. He revises the ideas, puts his own stamp on them, and by the time you come back to him with your report, he's three steps ahead and you just have to go along with it."

I *had* heard this before, but I thought that Carver had let up a bit in recent months. Apparently not. I didn't know what to say, so I said nothing. Hinde sighed, got up, and walked to the door. As she was leaving, she left this sentence hanging in the air: "If something isn't done about Carver, your product development team is going to implode."

Carver's Rise

I remembered the first time I saw Carver, nearly five years ago on a Saturday in November 1992. I was looking for a design engineer, and his background was perfect. He was one of those scholar-athletes: U.S. Junior National Ski Team, varsity football, avid fly fisherman. Engineering degree from Cal Tech and an M.B.A. from Stanford. Before Nuf Fun, he'd been working for three years at Trekkers, a hardware company in Silicon Valley. But he'd cashed in his stock options and bought a house in Boulder, a short drive from Nuf Fun's headquarters. Told me if he wasn't going to be home much, his family should at least live in a nice place. At the second interview, three days later, I asked him when he wanted to start, and he said, "Now."

When Carver came on board, we were having some trouble with our Sheer ski line. There had been record snowfalls during the 1991–1992 ski season, but our sales had been sluggish. In the spring, we did some customer surveys and discovered that people believed the

Sheer line was only for ski racers, cliff jumpers, and powder hounds. In late May, Carver came up with what became our best-selling Alpine skis, the Sheer Comfort, a range of midlength, softer boards for the Texans who come up to spend a few hours on the slopes and a few hours in the bar. His presentation was the best I'd ever seen: a solid product concept and ten pages of detailed analysis. In ten days, single-handed, he'd done the work of an entire development team. He'd even gotten someone in marketing to do a preliminary study on target markets and pricing.

Over the next three years, just about every new Nuf Fun product—such as our first in-line skates and our safety binding for water skis—bore Carver's initials. For our line of lightweight backpacks, Carver took anatomy classes and talked with sports medicine guys

---

Wooden claimed that the other engineers were feeling discouraged because Carver was riding roughshod over them.

---

to get the perfect weight distribution over the hips without stressing the shoulders. He even loaded the prototypes with 75-pound plates and hiked around

Estes Park for a couple of days. In 1994, the Comfort Trail won *Outside* magazine's Product of the Year award.

Carver could work for 15 hours without a break, and the amazing thing was, he never missed a detail; not a single figure or calculation was ever wrong. One time, he went two days straight without leaving the office or sleeping. When he let slip that he had seen a doctor about dizziness and chest pains, I sent him and his family for a week's R and R in the company condo on Dolphin Key. Every morning he was away, I found a fax waiting for me, each filled with ideas for what became the Scirocco, our line of high-performance windsurfing boards.

In late 1993, there were grumblings that Carver was tough to work with. Jim Wooden was still the head of product development back then, and Carver reported directly to him. During the Nuf Fun Christmas weekend at Snowcrest Peak that year, Wooden caught up with me at the bottom of the Devil's Drop triple chairlift, and all the way to the summit he warned me to take a good look at what Carver's overzealousness was doing to the department. He claimed that the other engineers were feeling discouraged because Carver was riding roughshod over them. He said that two of them had been out to talk to Boarding Sports, one of our biggest competitors.

One of my New Year's resolutions in 1994 was to check out the climate in product development. I did some walking around, and though morale did seem a little low, it didn't seem any worse than it ever does in the winter. In February, I brought in Verity Hinde at the same level as Carver. She had a solid design background and a reputation as a real team builder. Mainly, I was hoping that she would perk up the place.

In April, Wooden spent one afternoon with Kate Clarke, our head of human resources, and another with Clarke and me, reiterating his concerns about morale. At Nuf Fun, the HR function is really more of an administrative department than a full-fledged resource, so in May, on Clarke's advice, I called People Matters, a Denver HR consulting group, and set up a weeklong team-building workshop. We did some role-playing and an exercise called Moccasins, in which we had to stand in each other's shoes—literally—and vent our feelings. Wooden yelled at Carver for about ten minutes, which wasn't at all like him, and Hinde practically took Carver's ears off, but I saw them all in the bar later, laughing over a few beers.

On the last day of the workshop, we had to write a script of a typical transaction at the office. Most of us made a few rough notes and had a good laugh. Carver had his laptop and portable printer and put together a six-page story. The main character was a manager named John Pine who kept talking about relationships in the workplace during a concept meeting. It took me most of the next Monday to persuade Wooden to take back his resignation and another two hours to convince Carver that he'd stepped over the line. Things quieted down in the early summer, and I figured that was the end of it. I guess we see what we want to see.

Failing with Alacrity

Then we became involved in what has now euphemistically come to be called the "In-line Skate Wreck." We'd jumped into the in-line skate market in 1993 with a pair of generic skates: four wheels, a hinged shell, a padded innersole. Sales were within target. But in April 1994, our chief competitor, Sierra Express, came out with a five-wheel prototype that had a soft lining that molded to your feet—an idea their developers had taken from their own line of ski boots. Jim Wooden thought that if we could get a five-wheeler out with a better set of bearings and a more comfortable fit, we'd clear $5 million to $8 million in 1995.

I gave product development six weeks to get ready for a launch. In three weeks, the team found superlight bearings and a titanium housing, and used ski boot buckles and injection foam for a better fit. The blading season was in full swing, and we didn't have time for much testing. Wooden gave me the green light for launch. Carver raised hell, saying, for once, that we were moving too fast, but I figured he was just steamed because Wooden had dominated the design process. Carver had come up with his own design, as usual, but this time Wooden had overruled him. Hinde made a few noises as well, but I knew that she admired Carver's work, so I didn't pay much attention. We got the new skates to market by early June—we called them Alacrity.

Early sales were strong. But by mid-July, distributors were calling in with complaints. The Alacrity was the fastest skate on the market, but the rubber brake pads wore down much faster than those on competitors' skates. Even worse, the foam we were injecting into the inner boots had been designed for ski boots; in summer temperatures, the skates were just too hot to wear. The whole thing was a fiasco, and when the board saw the sales figures—and the amount of money we had spent to get out of the whole thing and do damage control—they pressured me into letting Wooden go.

Carver was the obvious choice to replace him. He already *was* the de facto head of the department. At our first meeting in late August, I told him that I wanted to see us double the number of new-product ideas, from 75 a year to at least 150. He said if we didn't hit 225, I could fire him. I reminded him that the snowboard market was heating up and that if he didn't have our new boards out by late October, I'd fire him, and if we ever had a repeat of the Alacrity, I'd fire him twice. On the way out, he picked up the lighted globe I keep by the door, put his right index finger on Nepal, and said, "I won't say I told you so about Alacrity. And as far as the half-pipes go, I'll get the best possible boards out by October 10, even if I have to carry them up Mount Everest alone to test them."

Two weeks later, he brought in Steve Bellmer and Janet Falkan, two 20-something, hot-ticket designers. At brainstorming meetings, Falkan even outtalked Carver. Hinde seemed restored by the new blood, and together, the four of them were unbeatable. True to Carver's word, Nuf Fun's freestyle boards were in the shops by October 8.

Before Christmas, Carver came up with new product-development policy, including a new vision for the department and a set of formal procedures (supported by various forms) that broke down the product development process into seven definable steps: idea, preliminary assessment, concept, development, testing, trial, and launch. He said he set up the policy so that everyone in the department could learn from him—and from one another. For the first time, everyone in and out of product development understood how Nuf Fun was going to gather new ideas, pick the best ones, and get them to market. It seemed like a great system.

Caution: Moguls Ahead

Of course, things are never completely hunky-dory in any business. Now and again, a junior engineer or designer griped that Carver wasn't setting clear goals or making his expectations clear. Hinde claimed that the junior people were capable, just not as compulsive as Carver. Bellmer came by one afternoon and said he was tired of working 70-hour weeks and not even getting a pat on the back. At a product brainstorming session I went to, Falkan just stared into her coffee cup as if she were reading the grounds.

Around that time, I read the theory that behavior is a function of personality and environment. I came down on the side of personality and decided that Carver could use some coaching. Kate Clarke of human resources agreed. I planned to bring it up at Carver's next review.

The morning of the review, Carver bounded into my office and plunked down a stack of printouts on the desk between us. They were covered with pencil and pen notations, arrows and crossed-out patches. For the first few minutes, he prowled aimlessly around my office. Then he leaned against the wall and rested his hands on his thighs. "Tough day," he said. "I'm not in the shape I used to be in."

I turned toward him and said, "Linus, you're the best I've ever seen, but I'm concerned that maybe you're trying to do too much yourself."

He took a big gulp of air. "Vic, don't come at me with that HR guru stuff again."

"You won't do me any good rigged up to an EKG."

"This is a break-heart business. You say it yourself. Nuf Fun has got to get its products out faster than Sierra Express and Boarding Sports and all the others, and they've got to be better." He glanced at his watch.

"You're right, Linus, but that's not the point here."

"What is the point?" he said. He had a flat, don't-con-me tone.

"The point is I'm getting worried about Bellmer and Falkan. They're your people, Linus."

He straightened. "This is a high-turnover business."

"Not so high that we also need to lose Verity Hinde."

"What are you talking about?"

"She's done a lot behind the curtains to keep the rest of your troupe happy, and I'm worried that she's ready to walk."

I said, "You can't be the Lone Ranger forever." But it came out sounding kind of unconvinced.

"Why worry about that? I've got ten heavy hitters in my recruiting file." He waved his mechanical pencil at the calendar on my desk. "I can have any one of them in here in ten days' time."

"Recruiting isn't going to make a better team."

"Team. Team. Team. Team." He came over to my desk and set his hands flat on the blotter in front of me, so close I could see the ropy veins. "Let's be honest. You hired me because I do the work of a whole department. And I have. And we're making money."

I said, "You can't be the Lone Ranger forever." The problem was, I knew he was right, and it came out sounding kind of unconvinced.

He stepped back and crossed his arms. "Vic, when you brought me in, our earnings per share were hovering around $1.37. Now they're up around $1.55, and in 18 months I'll have them to $1.80. The Parabolic ski is going to be a success—the testers love it, the racers love it, I love it. I predict revenues of close to $25 million on it."

"What good will that do us if you're in intensive care and Hinde, Bellmer, and Falkan are history?"

He circled my desk and sat down. "I work out so hard every day, I'll probably die healthy. Hinde's okay. And the others know that there's no better place in this industry than Nuf Fun. They're not leaving."

Carver leaned backward and crossed his legs. I hunched forward over my desk. "I just want to be sure, Linus," I said. "That's why I want you to get some coaching."

He practically lunged from the chair to the shelf and picked up my copy of *The Winning Executive Coach* and waved it in front of me. "This is all hocus-pocus. You can't change people. I'm type A. Always. Ambitious. Adrenaline."

I had the feeling I was standing in front of an oncoming train. "What would happen," I said, "if you delegated more, showed your people more trust, stressed praise instead of criticism?"

"Simple. We wouldn't get two product lines out this year or next year, either." He came so near I could see the pores in his cheeks. "You and the board and the stakeholders want new products. That's the name of the game." He sat down again and seemed to relax a little.

I counted to ten. "What I want is to see you giving more early support, building on other people's ideas—"

"And kissing our market position good-bye." He was drumming his fingers on his thigh. "What do you think the product development procedures are all about? You know I put them in place to help people learn. Look, I've got to get off to a meeting. I'll do what you say, and I'll meet with the coach. Is there anything else?"

I said no and escorted him to the door. He shook my hand and said, "I've got this great idea for a parachute jumpsuit with a built-in heater. You'll have the details on your desk Monday."

The bleating of my phone brought me back to the present. It was Bellmer. He seemed pretty ripped, so I just let him talk. He said he'd gone to Carver two weeks ago with an idea for in-line skating equipment—reflective knee and elbow pads, helmets, windbreakers with reflecting stripes—and Carver had just said, "Run with it." Bellmer was talking so fast, the words were running together, and it was giving me a headache. He went on, saying that at this week's new-product meeting, Carver had handed out plans for his own version. I rubbed my temples with my forefingers and tried to listen. I told Bellmer maybe that was good because they had two versions to discuss. That was when he said: "Discuss? We spent an hour discussing why my ideas weren't going to fly, and then another hour agreeing with Carver on how we were going to develop and test *his* reflecting ankle bands and wristbands." I asked him if maybe he wasn't overreacting a little, and then I heard that clumsy plastic clatter of the phone hanging up.

Sitting here, I have this feeling I'm up against the wall. If you look at the numbers, Nuf Fun is in great shape; if you look at the products, the development department is in great shape; and if you look at the people, Carver is in great shape. Without Carver, nothing will be in great shape. You know the old saying, If it ain't broke, don't fix it? Is anything really broken?

What, If Anything, Does Vic Need to Do About Carver?

Four experts discuss ways of handling brilliant, difficult individuals within an organization.

➤ Victor Vroom

Victor Vroom is John G. Searle Professor of Organization and Management and professor of psychology at the Yale School of Management in New Haven, Connecticut.

In real life, one is unlikely to find such extreme characters as Vic and Linus Carver. Vic is extraordinarily insensitive to what is happening in his product development department, and Carver is a superman in all respects but one. The man doesn't even need sleep! Having said that, however, the two do illustrate a dilemma that is unfortunately quite common in one form or another in many companies: How should a manager deal with an employee who is both a tremendous asset and a tremendous liability?

If I were Vic, I wouldn't give up quite yet. There are a few things he can try to improve the situation. To begin, he should get some training in the art of active listening. He would do well to read up on Carl Rogers' theories. (See, for example, Carl R. Rogers and F.J. Roethlisberger, "Barriers and Gateways to Communication," HBR July-August 1952.) Then he should have a thoughtful conversation with Carver. Yes, they've talked in the past—even about Carver's management style—but in each of those dialogues, Vic has given advice. He hasn't listened. Carver talks about being tired, and he's already had one possible heart attack. Those are indications that he is hurting, and they have gone right over Vic's head.

Even though Carver boasts about being able to hire heavy hitters, he may be frustrated with the people he has around him. He may not relish the managerial role in which he has been placed. He may, in fact, want to give up that role, but he may not see a way to get out and stay at Nuf Fun without losing face. What kind of role would Carver like to play? How does he see his career playing out? We don't know, because Vic hasn't truly tried to find out.

If Vic is able to find out where Carver stands, and if none of my speculations prove true, Vic must take a different tack. He needs to have a second dialogue with Carver in which the two examine the facts on which their inferences are based and attempt to come up with a mutually agreed-upon plan of action. In that conversation, Vic must play a stronger role than he has in the past, letting Carver know that he expects change, not simple acquiescence. "I'll do what you say, and I'll meet with the coach" won't wash if it isn't sincere. For this part of the process, I would recommend that Vic read the work of Chris Argyris. It's time he was introduced to double-loop learning, walking down the ladder of inference, and engaging in productive inquiry—concepts that could serve him well. (See, for example, "Teaching Smart People How to Learn," HBR May-June 1991.)

Either or both of these dialogues could lead to a solution. The first conversation may result in Carver saying, "Pay me what I'm worth, Vic, but I've had it. I'm not a manager." What sweet music that would be to everyone's ears. The second might lead to personal and professional growth for both of them.

I don't have a lot of faith in Vic's ability to pull this off. He is incredibly insensitive. There were signs when Jim Wooden was head of product development that Carver wasn't the managerial type, but Vic plowed right ahead with his appointment. All along, Verity Hinde looked more like a manager—she could have capitalized on Carver's talents, for which she has considerable respect. And she probably could have kept the peace in the department.

In any case, Vic may come out of this all right if he keeps one thing clear: his internal debate shouldn't focus only on whether to fire Carver or to keep him as a one-man band. The issues are never that black and white. Even in fiction.

➤ June Rokoff

June Rokoff is a director of Mathsoft, based in Cambridge, Massachusetts, and of Desktop Data, based in Burlington, Massachusetts. She is a former senior vice president of Lotus Development Corporation.

Vic doesn't have to do anything about Carver—at least not right now. So what if Carver's management skills are weak-to-nonexistent and his social skills are poor? In Carver, Vic has a guru who meets most of the requirements of the perfect product-development leader. Ask any CEO to describe the ideal candidate for that position and you're likely to hear: "a visionary; a creative person;

someone who understands both the business and marketing; someone with a proven track record on shipping products; a passionate, driven, dedicated person who is able to meet deadlines; someone who can recruit top talent." That's Carver all over.

Nuf Fun is in a great position. It has enviable sales growth, leading-edge products, and a product development team that must be the envy of other CEOs. If I were Vic—with his personality, his outlook, and his own shortcomings—I would probably sit tight.

Even if Vic wanted to "do something" about Carver, chances are he couldn't—at least not without doing something about himself first. In fact, the current arrangement at Nuf Fun is probably the only one that will work, given Vic's management style. This CEO is certainly hands off when it comes to development. In the course of his tenure, he has not developed a relationship with any of the other members of the product development department. He doesn't know firsthand what most of them are thinking; he doesn't even know where their talents lie. He may even have another Carver in the ranks, but he hasn't a clue. Vic can talk about the team concept, but he himself doesn't possess the skills to execute it successfully. He doesn't even have a cohesive management team—witness his human resources manager, who is relegated to an administrative role.

To his credit, Vic knows that the culture at Nuf Fun leaves a lot to be desired. What he doesn't seem to understand, however, is that it is the CEO's job to set the corporate culture and then to live in that culture. If Vic were to commit himself to changing the culture at Nuf Fun, he would have a lot of work to do.

- First, to create a culture that is inclusive, team oriented, and diverse, Vic would have to remove Carver from the pedestal on which he himself has placed him.

- Second, he would have to get professional help to learn how to create and participate in the kind of culture he wants the company to have. "Walking around" once, as he did in 1994, isn't going to cut it.

- Third, he would have to assemble a strong management team and learn to work with it on issues and goals involving people, just as he does on financial objectives and product development goals.

- Fourth, he would need a director of human resources who could help guide the culture so that, for example, an action plan and new goals and processes—monitored on an ongoing basis—would be developed following a retreat such as the company's team-building workshop.

- Finally, he should ask Carver to change. But he'd have to stop giving Carver mixed signals—on the one hand, telling him to listen to his team, and on the other, threatening to fire him if his products are late. Despite his faint protests, Vic is reinforcing Carver's behavior.

In the new culture, Carver would have to learn to delegate and to allow products to be developed with less of his imprint. He would have to learn how to give credit to others—and the value of doing so. I don't think that change is beyond Carver, contrary to his own opinion. But I do believe that the only way Vic could persuade Carver to change would be to show Carver that he himself was changing and that such change would be better for the company. We've seen that Carver is highly motivated by the success of the company; that message of success is the one Vic would have to deliver. (Vic might also consider finding a mentor for Carver—someone who has made the transition from developer to manager and understands the benefits of that move.)

A full-scale change of culture at Nuf Fun would be a roller-coaster ride for the company. Vic might be able to smooth the ride by putting Carver in the role of chief designer, with senior-level responsibility for product direction and leadership but no day-to-day responsibilities for managing a department. But even that move might take a year or more to work out. Vic would have to make sure that Carver believed he could still make a major contribution and that the company wouldn't stumble without him in his current role.

Carver is an asset under any scenario. And if Vic does nothing, the company will probably continue to grow for three, five, even ten years—for as long as Carver stays healthy. But a final word of caution: Carver's performance is not infinitely sustainable. Neither is his ability to recruit top talent. His health may fail, and, as word of his reputation spreads, his power to draw talented people to the company will erode. Moreover, Carver's output—two product lines per year—may not always be enough to outpace the competition. So even if Vic chooses the easy course, he must be aware that the company's growth won't continue forever. If nothing else, Vic needs to get to know the other people in the product development department. Developers are usually loyal to a product or a person but not to a company. Vic needs to find out what will keep his other talented employees engaged and work to gain their loyalty.

Incidentally, it's time for one of those talented people—Hinde—to evaluate her career. She's not using her team-building skills, and she gets no credit for product development. It's clear that she does not have Vic's ear; he's only humoring her. The longer she stays at Nuf Fun, the more her value erodes. It's time to move on.

➤ David Olsen

David Olsen is president and chief executive officer of Patagonia, based in Ventura, California.

No company the size of Nuf Fun can afford to be dependent on any one person. Such dependency puts the company at risk, stunts the development of its people, and limits the creativity brought to design and marketing opportunities.

What if Nuf Fun were to lose Carver suddenly? The company would be in crisis. Who knows if the other designers would be able to rise to the occasion; the company's culture has not prepared them to do so. Vic has a bigger problem on his hands than he thinks. He should focus his angst—and his efforts—on changing the company's entire culture to one that encourages innovation from every employee. Everyone in product development at Nuf Fun needs to have the opportunity to run with his or her own ideas— for better or for worse. Only in that kind of a culture can a star like Carver exist without posing a serious threat to the organization.

Of course, ending the dependence on Carver and changing Nuf Fun's corporate culture is no easy task—particularly for a CEO who doesn't yet understand the scope of the problem. Vic knows that Nuf Fun needs a team-based culture. But despite his statements to the contrary, Vic does not believe in teams. He hired Carver to do "the work of a whole department," and he does not see that his talk about a team approach conflicts with his reliance on Carver.

I don't know who at Nuf Fun is going to alert Vic to that conflict. But if we consider this his wake-up call, here's what he has to do, in both broad and specific terms:

- Place more emphasis on building the company to be successful over the long term. Right now, Vic is too concerned about short-term financial results. A team-based structure could help him position the company for long-term success. I suggest that Vic figure out what *team* really means and start thinking about how Nuf Fun would look if it really ran on team power.

- Work with his board of directors. If Vic and the directors don't support the team approach, it will fail.

- Balance Nuf Fun's demands for quality with its speed in getting products to market. The Alacrity fiasco shouldn't have happened in the first place, but when it did, Vic should have been all over the process afterward, figuring out what went wrong and assessing the steps that led to the disaster. Again, Vic's shortsightedness causes problems for his organization. He has done nothing to prevent such a mistake from happening again.

- Really listen to his employees. Vic must be willing to hear about and address any problems at Nuf Fun. As his conversation with Hinde demonstrates, he basks in the company's financial performance but ignores Nuf Fun's deeper problems.

- Position his human resources department to lead the transformation to a team-based culture. A company like Nuf Fun should not have a human resources department that serves little more than an administrative function. Building a department that can direct employee education and development will strengthen the organization.

- Base rewards and recognition on teamwork and development. For example, when a product succeeds, the rewards should go to everyone involved, including designers, engineers, and marketers—not simply to the lead designer. New ideas may come from individuals, but successful products—even Carver's—require a group effort.

- Reassign Carver to a position called senior design engineer, independent of the product development department. Carver is too valuable to lose, but he is not a team player or a manager. To make such a move attractive, Vic can offer Carver a small support staff and the autonomy to design and develop his own products, subject to the approval of the CEO and the director of development. If Carver is unwilling to accept the position, Vic must let him leave. Carver is brilliant, but he is not more valuable than the entire product development group.

- Promote Hinde to director of product development. The change will make it clear that there is a new management direction, a new structure, and a new culture at Nuf Fun. Hinde's promotion will help morale among the other employees, especially Steve Bellmer and Janet Falkan. Given her reputation, it will also send the message that teamwork is now valued within a framework that allows individuals to think creatively.

Nuf Fun is positioned to be very successful for the next few years. There's no better time for Vic to change his thinking and for Nuf Fun to change its structure. The level of risk is as low as it is going to get. Vic should not wait.

➤ David H. Burnham

David H. Burnham is a partner in the Burnham Rosen Group, a consulting firm based in Boston, Massachusetts, that specializes in leadership training, executive coaching, and business strategy.

As Hinde says (paraphrasing Vic), "One of Nuf Fun's real big advantages is its diversity—not one single product category accounts for more than 15% of overall sales." Diversity is a prudent strategic principle. Vic should apply it to his employees as well. Right now, he is at risk of reducing his product development staff to one: Carver. Hinde, Bellmer, and presumably Falkan—all people Carver himself admits are very talented—are seriously unhappy. Keeping Carver just isn't worth losing everyone else.

Although Vic seems to know that, he is reluctant to admit it. His reticence will be his downfall. Unless he makes more than a halfhearted attempt to get Carver to change, he will have only himself to blame when the company is in a shambles some years down the road.

In fact, Vic's lack of action is laying the groundwork for just such a disaster. If things remain the same, most of his talented engineers and designers are likely to leave—

perhaps to strengthen the competition. If they stay, they will become increasingly disgruntled and unmotivated, soaking up time and resources but producing little.

Carver isn't a superman with a lifetime guarantee, either. Without a supportive staff, his stream of ideas will eventually dry up or lose relevance; he is already stealing ideas from his subordinates and marketing them as his own. And he cannot and will not be right all the time. The question isn't, Will Carver's judgment eventually cause a product development failure? The questions are, When will such a failure happen? and How much will it cost Nuf Fun? Of course, Carver may leave Nuf Fun before he causes that kind of disaster. He enjoys competing, and at Nuf Fun he has created (perhaps unconsciously) a situation in which he can compete with his own staff. If his staff leaves him, Carver will become bored and begin to look for another place where he can compete internally as well as in the marketplace. Either way, Nuf Fun loses.

Vic reports that his one plan to date—to persuade Carver to get some executive coaching—comes from his understanding of a theory about behavior being a function of personality and environment. So he has decided to work on Carver's personality. But Vic needs to deal with both parts of the equation if there is to be any change in Carver's behavior.

Consider the environment from Carver's point of view. How does he perceive Vic's expectations for his behavior, and what are his incentives? Right now, Carver believes that Vic has only two expectations: that Carver's products win in the marketplace and that he keep the number of new-product ideas high regardless of the process. Vic has not been persuasive about his desire to foster teamwork; Carver knows that Vic's heart isn't in it. So the only clear incentives Carver has are disincentives: Meet product deadlines or be fired. Don't have a disaster like Alacrity or be fired twice. If Vic expects Carver to change his approach, Vic must change his own behavior as well. He must set new expectations and incentives as well as provide coaching for Carver to enable him to learn and understand the appropriate behaviors.

I would recommend that Vic do the following:

- Tell Carver—clearly and firmly—that he not only believes in teamwork but also wants and expects Carver to create an effective team.

- Tell Carver that his assumptions are wrong. He cannot continue to be a one-man band, because business results will inevitably decline.

- Let Carver know that the strategic risks for Nuf Fun are too great for the company to be too dependent on any one person. Let him know that it is irresponsible to insist on operating the way he does and that it would be irresponsible of Vic to tolerate the current situation any longer.

- Try to make Carver understand that building a team requires him to realize the goals of the process he himself created. Product development cycles won't stall if he sticks to the process; rather, the process will ensure steady, focused development.

- Tell Carver that it was both unacceptable and discouraging to "improve" Bellmer's idea. Let him know that it must not happen again, and ask him to accept responsibility for his behavior and apologize to Bellmer.

Vic should offer Carver a compensation package in which 50% of Carver's variable pay would be based on the product development group's results and 50% on Carver's management of the team. His performance on the latter should be measured by the diversity of ideas generated and accepted and by employee satisfaction levels, which should be assessed through formal feedback mechanisms.

If Carver does not agree to these terms, Vic should ask for his resignation. The risks of keeping him without any change far outweigh those of losing him.

If he agrees, then Vic, together with Carver's new coach, should carefully plan an immediate meeting with the product development staff. Following the principle that public acknowledgment increases commitment to change, Carver should apologize to Bellmer and, with Vic, establish the new commitment to teamwork.

Vic must also announce that he will be meeting with Carver and his team every two weeks to review product development progress and processes. He should monitor morale for several months, until he is certain that Carver is established in his new behavior. If team spirit hasn't improved after three months (and assuming that business results remain steady or improve), Vic should replace Carver with Hinde. Hinde may be able to employ Carver in a "special assignment" in which he would assume sole responsibility for particular product-development tasks. That option is fraught with risks, however, not the least of which would be that Carver might sabotage his colleagues' work. Carver would have to agree to keep away from over-all product development, and Vic would need to reinforce that separation. If Carver balked at that plan or failed to abide by the new terms, then again, I would recommend that Vic let him go.

Originally published in July–August 1997

Reprint 97401

EILEEN ROCHE

Do Something—

He's About to Snap

Executive Summary

Lynne Tabor, an IT manager at manufacturing giant MMI, has a great team. Everyone works hard and gets along. Everyone, that is, except Max Dyer. Max is a talented programmer, but he's terrible in the interpersonal skills department. So terrible, in fact, that three years ago Lynne reworked his job after employees complained that he was unengaged and even belligerent.

Since then, he's been a solid worker, putting in extra hours and meriting good performance evaluations. But recently, Max's coworkers have noticed a change for the worse in him. True, everyone at MMI is on edge after a round of layoffs, but Max's behavior seems like more than a case of the jitters. To make matters worse, reports of a workplace shooting in Seattle are all over the news. Paige overhears Max shouting at someone on the phone. George finds Max pinning up a certificate from a shooting range in his cubicle, and Nicole, who worries they will all end up as statistics of office violence, wants to know how Lynne plans to ensure their safety.

When Lynne tries to talk to Max, it's clear he thinks his coworkers are out to get him. And the truth is, they believe he fits the profile of a man on the edge. But what can Lynne do about an employee who has never made so much as a veiled threat to anyone?

Commentators James Alan Fox, a professor of criminal justice at Northeastern University; Steve Kaufer, a cofounder of the Workplace Violence Research Institute; Christine Pearson, a management professor at Thunderbird; Christine Porath, a professor of management and organizational behavior at the University of Southern California's Marshall School of Business; and Ronald Schouten, the director of the Law and Psychiatry Service at Massachusetts General Hospital, offer advice in this fictional case study.

"Guess who I ran into at CVS last night?" Nicole Ianucci paused for effect, then leaned in toward her coworkers. "Max was there, in line at the prescription counter. I couldn't see what he was picking up, but you know what I think? I think he's having some sort of a breakdown. That would explain why he's been acting so weird lately."

"Oh, come on, Nicole," Derek scoffed. "The poor guy probably has a cold, and you've got him on antipsychotics. This is how rumors get started."

"I know everyone around here thinks I'm a drama queen," she whispered, "but honestly, doesn't he give you the creeps? I mean, I used to think he was just a harmless oddball, but haven't you noticed he's getting worse—like, ever since last Tuesday?"

No one had to be reminded of the significance of last Tuesday. That was the day a disgruntled office worker in Seattle had walked into his workplace, a .38-caliber pistol in each hand, and shot several coworkers before turning one of the guns on himself. Nicole continued, "These things always set off copycats. And they go interview the guy's neighbors, and it's always the same: 'He kept to himself,' or 'He was kind of a misfit.' Does that sound like anyone we know?"

As if on cue, Max Dyer walked by, ducking his head and concealing as best he could a paper plate bending under the weight of three bagels. It was easy to imagine this tall, awkward man as the kid nobody wanted to

---

"Doesn't he give you the creeps? I mean, I used to think he was just a harmless oddball, but haven't you noticed he's getting worse?"

---

play with back in grade school. His beard needed trimming, his shirt was untucked, there were coffee stains on his pants, even the lenses of his glasses were speckled with dirt. When he was out of earshot, Nicole arched her brow and continued, "The man will not even make eye contact. I'm telling you, he's a freak."

"And what's with the stockpiling of food?" Paige chimed in. "He's always lurking around the kitchen, just waiting to scavenge any leftovers someone drops off after a meeting. I mean, really, have some self-respect."

Derek shrugged. "Okay, he is a little strange. I'll give you that. But guys, lighten up. So he's got a big appetite, and he's cheap—big deal. We've all got quirks. The fact is, he's a great programmer. Everybody's on edge because of all the layoff talk around here. Cut him some slack, would you?"

As Lynne Tabor walked toward the watercooler, she noticed three of her top programmers engrossed in conversation. Normally, she'd have thought nothing of it, but something about their expressions gave her pause. Nicole had that "sky is falling" look on her face, and Paige appeared to be annoyed. Derek seemed calm enough, but then, he was possibly the most laid-back man on the planet. "Please don't let Nicole be stirring up layoff rumors again," Lynne thought. "Morale's been low enough since the last round." Smiling brightly, she approached the group. "Hi, guys. What's up?"

They exchanged pleasantries, talked about the school play Nicole's daughter was in, and vented their horror at the Seattle shooting, which was all over the news. The conversation wound down with a status report on Derek's current project. In short, everything seemed fine, but Lynne had a nagging feeling that she was missing something.

Odd Man Out

The recession had hit manufacturing giant MMI hard, Lynne reflected as she walked back to her office, and people were understandably jittery. Originally called

Mailing Machines International, the company's name had been shortened 30 years ago when it expanded into other electronic office equipment. MMI had been good to Lynne: She'd started as an intern and was hired as a full-time programmer when she graduated from college. A few years ago, she was promoted into management. After 15 years at MMI, Lynne cared a great deal about the company, and particularly about her staff. But if MMI missed its quarterly targets again, there might very well be a second round of layoffs.

Lynne's unit had already lost two people, both of whom qualified for the early retirement package. But that meant the others had to pick up extra work, and long hours had become the norm. Luckily for her, Lynne had great people on her team—they worked hard, they helped each other out, and everyone seemed to get along. Everyone except Max, that is.

Max Dyer had a strong work ethic; she couldn't fault him there. He was always in the office before she got in at 7:00, and he was still there when she left most evenings. She was concerned about burnout with that sort of schedule, but the one time she brought it up with him, he had answered in his typical monosyllabic style. When she pressed him, he said he was fine and then asked if that was all she needed and if he could get back to work. Max was not one for idle chat.

In fact, he was pretty terrible in the "interpersonal skills" department—so bad that three years ago his position had to be reworked. According to his original job description, he was supposed to work with the engineers who designed MMI's mailing machines—he created software that mapped out the plans for assembling the parts. The plans were accessed at workstations by the workers on the production floor who built the equipment. The job itself was complex—no question—and Max had to field questions and revision requests from both the engineers and the production workers. But soon enough, both groups began asking Lynne to assign someone other than Max to their projects. They couldn't fault the quality of his work, exactly, but neither could they warm up to him as a collaborator. According to the engineers, in meetings at which he was supposed to be eliciting their requirements, he sat silent and let them do all the talking. It wasn't clear he was even listening, they complained, because his few comments were often non sequiturs. And when he did make a valuable contribution, it took some doing to find the thread between what he was saying and the topic at hand. The production workers were just as unhappy: They thought he talked down to them. When they pointed out problems with the plans—such as the schematic appearing on a different screen than the assembly instructions—he turned defensive, even belligerent.

Lynne remembered well the awkward conversation she'd had with Max at the time. His fidgeting and obvious unease in response to a series of questions about people and projects satisfied her that these weren't specific personality clashes; Max was socially inept across the board. So Lynne appeased the engineers and production workers by assigning Paige to their projects and managed to retain Max's programming expertise by rewriting his job description to call for less interaction with users. It seemed like the perfect solution at the time, especially considering that the whole IT industry was engaged in a war for talent. Paige was a winner, too, since her expanded role merited a raise.

Lynne was proud of the way she had handled that problem, despite some initial reservations she'd had about Max's compensation. Ideally, she would have reduced his salary to reflect the scaled-back nature of his job. But that, she knew, would have been adding insult to injury, and Max seemed more than a little humiliated about what others would perceive as a demotion. In the end, he had deserved the pay, anyway. He drove himself hard, increased his output, and got good performance reviews.

Lynne did worry that he had become even more antisocial, perhaps because his job no longer forced him to interact with people on a regular basis. Max never went to lunch with the other people on his team, and it was rare to hear him discuss weekend plans or current events with anyone. But she had more pressing concerns than one wallflower programmer. The most important thing was to keep the whole team focused and motivated.

Growing Unease

"You don't like pickles, do you?" Paige asked as she reached across to Nicole's lunch tray.

"Help yourself," Nicole replied. "I'm not really hungry, anyway. I'm worried sick about the whole Max thing."

"What's the 'whole Max thing'?" asked Sam, another programmer in their group. "Wait, don't tell me: He's wearing those sandals you hate so much, is that it?"

"She's convinced he's going to snap and take us all out with him. Isn't that right, Nic?"

"It's easy to laugh, Derek, and I hate to say it, but what if she's on to something?" asked George, one of the engineers. "Get this. I stopped by Max's cubicle the other day to drop off some printouts, and what do I find him doing? Pinning up a certificate from some shooting range. I guess he's been getting in some practice."

Paige's eyes widened. "Oh, my God!"

Sam hastened to calm her. "Hey, come on. I've been known to spend some time at the range. If you're a hunter . . ." But a note of uncertainty crept into his voice.

Paige jumped back in. "Did any of you hear him lose it on the phone last week? I don't know who he was talking to, but he totally flipped out. I swear, I thought he was going to hurl something across the room. Then he slammed down the receiver and just stormed out. It was scary."

"Hey, at least now we know that he does leave the building sometimes," Derek said, trying to lighten the mood. But it didn't work. Sam was starting to look as jumpy as the rest of them.

"Yeah," he said slowly. "Why is he always in the office? It's like he lives here now. Maybe that explains the stash of food at his desk."

"You know, I've stopped coming in most week-ends," Paige admitted sheepishly. "I know we've got a ton of work to do before the next rollout, George—and I'll get it done, I will—but I just can't stand the thought of being here all alone with Max. It skeeves me out. He's got that 'bodies stashed in the basement' sort of look to him, doesn't he?"

Nicole scanned the table. "I'm not so crazy after all, am I? I'm telling you, Max is on the edge. And I don't want to end up a statistic."

An Unsettling Meeting

Lynne took a deep breath before launching into the explanation of why she had called Max into her office. "One of your coworkers has expressed some concern about you, Max. Apparently there was an incident last Thursday with a phone call?"

Max's head jerked back, almost as if he had taken a physical blow, and when he met her eye she was surprised at the intensity of his stare. She swallowed. "It sounds like you were extremely angry."

Max's expression turned to a sarcastic sneer. "Oh? They've been telling you things about my performance? Why doesn't that surprise me?"

It quickly became clear that Max believed the people around him were conspiring to make him look bad, if not to undermine his work outright. It made sense, he pointed out to Lynne. Layoffs were looming, and his output was higher than theirs. "The rats," he said, "are beginning to panic."

For the next several minutes, Lynne tried to get to the root of his suspicion and assure him that no one wanted the team's performance to be compromised. But as she talked, she saw him regarding her carefully. At some point it occurred to her that he was trying to size her up. Was she on his side—or theirs?

As she closed the door behind him, she drew her first deep breath since the conversation had started. "My God," she thought, "that's real paranoia."

"And yet," she admitted to herself, "Max is absolutely right: They are out to get him."

Time for Action?

Lynne wasn't sure what to make of it, she explained to Gene Kozlowski, the vice president of human resources. Layoff anxiety she was ready for. And feelings of burnout? Yeah, those were expected, too. But fear for one's personal safety? She hadn't seen that one coming.

Gene took a swig of coffee. "Okay, let's have it. What's going on with Max? Last I heard, he was doing well ever since we took him off the process plans."

Lynne started by recapping the conversation she had had with Nicole the day before. A visibly upset Nicole had walked into her office and claimed that she was scared that Max might become violent. She had also said that Paige and Sam, as well as George in engineering, shared her concerns, and they wanted to know what Lynne was prepared to do to ensure their safety. Lynne had assured her that safety was, of course, her primary concern and then had asked Nicole to explain why she felt threatened. Nicole had listed a host of reasons, and Lynne had thanked her for her honesty and had promised to think seriously about what the next steps should be.

The problem was, none of Nicole's reasons held up very well under scrutiny. Even Nicole had admitted that Max had never made so much as a veiled threat to anyone in the office. Yes, he owned a gun, but so did lots of other MMI employees. He was definitely a loner, but was that really an indicator of future violent behavior? The fact that he had bought some type of prescription drug was hardly worth considering—except that it reminded Lynne that she needed to pick up her allergy pills on the way home. And that "explosive" phone call, as Nicole put it? Well, one outburst wasn't grounds for dismissal, which seemed to be what Nicole was looking for. Moreover, Lynne couldn't ignore the fact that Nicole had a well-known flair for the dramatic—she joked about it herself at times. Was this another case of her blowing things out of proportion?

On the other hand, the fact that Paige—and maybe others—had stopped working late or on weekends to avoid being alone with Max was a definite cause for

---

"Isn't part of being professional learning how to deal with all sorts of people, even those who make you uncomfortable?"

---

concern. And Nicole was right when she pointed out that people here used the same words to describe Max that employees at that Seattle company had used to describe their gunman coworker. And Max *had* been looking more disheveled lately.

Lynne explained to Gene that after her meeting with Nicole, she had talked with Max about his coworkers' concerns. But instead of feeling reassured by their conversation, she had ended up feeling more anxious.

Her thoughts took another turn. "Isn't part of being a professional learning how to deal with all sorts of people, even those who make you uncomfortable?" she asked Gene. "It's not as if I'm asking Nicole and the others to *like* Max. I've got to think of the big picture here. What would happen if we did decide to get rid of him and he hired an attorney? Do we want to go down that road? But if we don't take action and something tragic happens—I just couldn't live with myself. I don't want to be the next workplace violence story on the news."

Lynne trailed off and shrugged. "So that's where things stand. I'm at a loss, Gene. I just don't see an easy fix—or even a hard fix," she smiled wanly. "I don't want anyone to feel like they're at risk, but I don't see how we can take action against a guy who hasn't done anything wrong."

Is Max a Threat?

Five commentators offer expert advice.

➤ James Alan Fox

James Alan Fox is the Lipman Family Professor of Criminal Justice at Northeastern University in Boston.

In the wake of any episode of workplace vengeance, like the Seattle shooting described in this case study, employees in companies near and far commonly identify with the victims. More than just sympathizing, they may fear that similar rampages could occur within their own organizations.

The media reports that everyone at MMI is hearing are probably sprinkled with suggestions of an epidemic of workplace violence and most likely include some alarming statistics. Homicide is the leading cause of workplace fatalities for women, and second for men; more than 1,000 workers die each year in homicides on the job. The message is painfully clear: You had better watch out, because the next mass murderer may be working in your office! In this kind of hypersensitive climate, is it any wonder that Max Dyer is so frightening to his colleagues?

The scary statistics cited in newspapers and magazines are quite misleading, however. The vast majority of workplace homicides and assaults are the result of robberies at retail stores or of taxi drivers. Of the millions of Americans in the labor force, a few dozen die each year at the hands of disgruntled colleagues. There is a risk, to be sure, but a miniscule one.

Of course, there are reasonable steps we can take to make that risk even smaller—whether or not a layoff is coming, whether or not there is someone like Max around to stir up emotions and rumors. But it is important not to make the situation worse out of fear and panic.

Many supervisors try to minimize the risk of workplace violence by looking for warning signs, comparing employees with profiles found in books, pamphlets, and on the Internet. The typical workplace avenger is a reclusive, middle-aged white male who feels that his job and financial well-being are in jeopardy. Facing yet another disappointment or failure at work, he senses that his career is slipping away. He also believes that he is not to blame. Rather, it's the supervisor who gives him poor assignments or doesn't appreciate his hard work; it's his coworkers who get all the credit when profits go up; it's the human resources personnel who are out to get him.

Max's colleagues have surely spent too much time studying this profile. Undoubtedly, Max does exhibit certain disturbing characteristics. As a loner, he lacks the support systems that most of us depend on to help us cope with adversity. His long hours at the office suggest that he devotes too much of himself to his job and not enough to hobbies and other outside activities. Problems tend to arise when work is the only meaningful part of someone's life. Fortunately, Max has not indicated in any overt way that he is dangerous. His certificate of marksmanship may say more about what gives him a sense of pride than about any desire to harm his coworkers. Despite our wish to find safety in profiling, such prediction strategies are doomed to fail. Tens of thousands of disgruntled Americans in workplaces large and small are frustrated, never smile, and live alone. Yet very few will ever translate their inner feelings of anger into outward expressions of violence.

Treating Max like a ticking time bomb can actually do much more harm than good. If he senses that he is being targeted in a negative way, it could reinforce any feelings of persecution that he may already harbor. Singling him out could precipitate the violent outburst that it is designed to prevent.

The best strategy is to reach out to him, affirm his worth as an employee, try to involve him in group lunches and social events, and help him find balance in his life. These are the right things to do with all employees, not just the ones who scare us.

Ultimately, the best approach for reducing the risk of workplace violence is not to focus on the Max Dyers of the world—the oddballs, geeks, and misfits—but to focus on humanizing the entire workplace. Civility, respect, decency, and worker satisfaction must become a critical part of the bottom line.

➤ Steve Kaufer

Steve Kaufer is the cofounder of the Workplace Violence Research Institute in Palm Springs, California, and the coauthor of The Complete Workplace Violence Prevention Manual, *which was published by the institute in 1997 and is updated quarterly.*

After someone becomes violent in the workplace, people often come forward and say, "He was a nice guy, but . . .," and then they list all these disturbing things about him that they had never reported to anyone. That's why I think Max's coworkers have taken a positive step by airing their concerns to management.

That said, they may be reading too much into the situation. They're trying to apply a profile to Max, and profiles don't work. They are thinking that if he does certain things—if he fits the profile—they should be concerned.

But everybody has what you could call a baseline behavior. Max's baseline is being a little creepy and looking unkempt and wearing some of his lunch. That's not weird behavior for Max because he's always been that way. In most cases, the trouble starts only if the baseline behavior changes. Max's changes only a little in this case: He has one angry outburst, and he's started to spend more time at work—but perhaps he doesn't have a lot of outside interests or his workload is heavy. If it changes more dramatically—if his hair's going in 18 different directions and he looks like he slept in his car—then I would be concerned. For instance, I saw a situation in which a government employee moved out of his apartment and made no attempt to find another place to live. He used facilities at a campsite to clean himself up and slept in his car. His behavior said that he was not making any attempt to relocate, that perhaps he had other plans that would obviate the need for a long-term living solution.

Getting back to Max, Lynne Tabor has stumbled in the past by accommodating him rather than dealing with his unwanted behavior. She sent the message that it's okay for Max to be grumpy and cranky; the rest of the staff will work around him. She should counsel Max on his behavior. Chances are she'll find an underlying issue: a problem at home, an illness, the fact that he doesn't believe he's been treated fairly at work. If she can get to the heart of the matter, she'll be more likely to help him become a better colleague. But if she's walking on eggshells around him, afraid to take disciplinary action because she's scared he's going to do something, that's a huge problem.

Litigation is the outcome of almost every serious incident of workplace violence. In terms of liability, MMI is obligated to investigate now that it knows that employees are concerned about Max. If it doesn't, and Max does become violent, the plaintiff will use that information against MMI. On the other hand, the company might face a wrongful termination suit if it fires Max without building a proper case. Too often, especially when dealing with somebody who's a little weird, companies haven't built a strong case because nobody ever wanted to deal with the person. So when the last-straw incident occurs, there's nothing in the employee's personnel file. At that point, management either has to start from scratch or terminate the employee and hope the company doesn't get sued.

But in a case like this, particularly when the employee is fairly good—Max is performing his job, he's just strange—I think the company has to adopt more of a benevolent perspective than a punitive one. Lynne and Gene Kozlowski need to find out what's driving Max's behavior. They're never going to change his weirdness, but other issues have surfaced that seem to be getting worse: paranoia, anger, changes in his already odd appearance. Something is behind that, and they need to find out what. They should consider what MMI can do so that his behavior does not escalate. A lot of organizations have employee assistance programs (EAPs), for example, and they're great resources in situations like this. So, unless there has been a direct threat or a serious violation of company policy—like an assault or something else totally inexcusable—the best approach is the benevolent one. They should try to figure out what's going on with this guy and how to help him become a productive and collegial employee.

➤ Christine Pearson

Christine Pearson is an associate professor of management at Thunderbird, the American Graduate School of International Management, in Glendale, Arizona. Christine Porath is an assistant professor of management and organizational behavior at the University of Southern California's Marshall School of Business in Los Angeles.

Max's behavior is costing MMI big bucks, in ways the company probably doesn't realize. According to our research on incivility in the workplace, about one-quarter of those who have to interact with Max will cut back their hours—as Paige has done—and another quarter will intentionally reduce their effort. Additionally, roughly one-third of Max's coworkers will spread rumors and withhold information, another third will avoid him, and many will engage in organizational deviance, behavior that violates the norms of the workplace and is harmful to the organization, its members, or both. Some people will sabotage their bosses out of anger for not correcting the situation, and one in eight will actually change jobs—but they'll never tell you why.

Given those numbers, Lynne can't ignore the situation. But before she can deal with Max, she needs to take a look in the mirror. As a manager, Lynne has fallen short: She's harboring an uncivil employee, colluding with office gossip, and running scared. But encountering a workplace avenger is less likely than being struck dead by lightning. So while Lynne needs to address the fear that's brewing at MMI, her most pressing problem is that employee relations have run amok because she didn't deal with Max years ago. By giving him a new job description and great performance evaluations, she has reinforced his antisocial tendencies and fostered costly norms of incivility. Now she's afraid to act because Max might hire an attorney and because he just might live up to the rumors.

At this point, Lynne should involve others at MMI in creating a written statement about employee interactions. It can be as simple as "At MMI, employees treat one another with respect," and it can be folded into an existing mission or values statement. (The breadth of incivility in Lynne's department suggests that no such statement exists; if it does, Lynne is in trouble for not holding her subordinates accountable.) Even if MMI is not willing to set a company-wide norm, Lynne should do so in her division. Such a statement becomes a benchmark against which all uncivil behavior can be monitored and corrected before it damages organizational culture, employees, and customers.

Lynne should discuss three issues with Gene: creating the company policy, obtaining relevant details in Max's employment record that she may not be aware of, and enrolling Max in training programs to correct his interpersonal deficiencies. Lynne should then talk with the head of MMI's security to make employees' safety concerns known.

She should also request a confidential criminal background check on Max as a precaution.

To put a stop to the incivility in her own area, she must meet with her direct reports to stress the importance of the new policy and the consequences for those who violate it, regardless of their special competencies. She should institute 360-degree feedback to track how employees treat one another. Lynne should also tell Nicole, in private, that her behavior violates the new policy and that she will be held accountable.

Lynne must also meet again with Max. Since their last conversation failed to uncover the reason for his unprofessional phone encounter—the only misbehavior that she could have disciplined legitimately—she should revisit that topic. Then she must explain that he needs coaching and training from HR, and together they can establish a timetable. This discussion should be framed as an effort to help Max so that his technical abilities will not be held back by his interpersonal incompetence. Lynne must explain that the standards for coworker respect that apply to all employees also apply to him. She should document this meeting and add it to Max's personnel file as a contract and as evidence of a corporate attempt to correct the problem, should Max ever hire an attorney. If, after these steps, Max's uncivil behavior continues or escalates, he should be fired.

➤ Ronald Schouten

Ronald Schouten, a psychiatrist and attorney, is the director of the Law and Psychiatry Service at Massachusetts General Hospital in Boston and president of KeyPeople Resources, a consulting firm in Boston specializing in corporate health, disaster management, and behavioral health services.

Workplace homicides are rare, but when they occur, their devastating effects extend beyond the loss of individual life. Family members and coworkers are also victims, and the organization itself can experience serious business repercussions from lost productivity and a damaged public image. As if that weren't enough, the situation is a legal minefield.

It is not surprising that Max's behavior makes his coworkers nervous, especially given the layoffs and the workplace shooting in Seattle. Such events raise anxiety and often lead to a lot of talk about profiles. But if workplaces were to exclude all employees with commonly cited risk factors (white men, 30 to 50 years old, like to work alone, have trouble getting along with others, can't accept criticism), they'd be practically empty.

Is Max a threat? His deteriorating behavior, difficulty accepting criticism, angry outbursts, and accusations that others are out to harm him are all risk factors, as is his involvement with guns—but only because it proves he has access to weapons. The fact that Max has not threatened anyone is worth noting, but as research from the Secret

Service has shown, it's important to focus not on whether someone *makes* a threat but on whether he or she *poses* a threat.

That puts Lynne in a difficult, but not uncommon, situation. What if Max has a documented mental health condition? She might be tempted to delay taking action for fear of a suit under the Americans with Disabilities Act (ADA) or a state equivalent. The ADA makes it unlawful for employers to discriminate against individuals on the basis of a current or past physical or mental disability. It also prohibits discrimination against those perceived to have a disability, even if they do not. But appropriate workplace interventions and discipline can be applied to disabled individuals—they are subject to the same workplace rules as nondisabled employees. Max is unlikely to have an ADA claim if Lynne handles him the way she would any other employee who disrupted the workplace. Additionally, she might fear a wrongful termination or defamation lawsuit if Max is let go or is escorted out of the workplace and portrayed as dangerous.

But if Lynne does nothing, and Max acts out Nicole's worst fears, MMI could face negligent hire or negligent retention lawsuits. There may also be federal and state Occupational Safety and Health Administration (OSHA) citations for failure to maintain a safe workplace. In fact, the stress of the situation may lead employees to seek workers' compensation.

Even so, many managers are reluctant to intervene, either because they don't want to intrude into an employee's personal life or because they fear that their action will push the person over the edge. But most struggling employees respond positively to good-faith inquiries about their well-being. And the concern that your action will topple someone over the edge is actually the strongest argument for doing something.

My advice to Lynne is to ask Max again if he's all right, comment on his apparent stress level, and engage him as a fellow human being. The next steps depend on his response. Under the best circumstances, he will acknowledge that he does not get along with people. Under the worst circumstances, he will become hostile and threatening. Most interactions like this lie somewhere between these extremes.

Policy and procedures for cases like Max's are important: Workplaces should have teams—with representatives from management, HR, legal, mental health, security, and public relations—to handle such crises. More important still is the ability to strike a balance between fear and denial while addressing everyone's interests in an objective, concerned manner.

Originally published in July 2003

Reprint R0307A

When Salaries

Aren't Secret

Executive Summary

No one seemed to think Treece McDavitt was a malevolent employee. "Just mischievous," one person said.

Whatever her motivation, the day before Treece was to leave RightNow!, an off-price women's fashion retailer, the 26-year-old computer wizard accessed HR's files and e-mailed employees' salaries to the entire staff. Now everyone knows what everyone else is making; they are either infuriated that they are making too little or embarrassed that they are making too much. Salary disparities are out there for everyone to see, and CEO Hank Adamson has to do something to smooth things over.

Hank's trusted advisers talk extensively with the CEO about his options, ultimately coming down on two sides. Charlie Herald, vice president of human resources, takes a "You get a lemon, you make lemonade" approach: keep making the salaries public to ensure fairness to push employees to higher performance, he advises. Meanwhile, CFO Harriet Duval sees the need for damage control: apologize, clean up the company's compensation system, and continue to keep—or at least *try* to keep—salaries private, she says.

Should Hank side with Charlie or Harriet? Or perhaps find a compromise between their two views? What should he do about this serious salary debacle? Four commentators offer their advice on the problem presented in this fictional case study.

It had all happened so fast. Hunched forward, elbows on the desk, Hank let his chin sink deeper into his hands as he gazed out into the night. Outside, the flowers in the office-park garden looked garish under the orange sodium-vapor lights. Hank didn't notice. He was thinking hard about tomorrow's staff meeting, which had so suddenly been transformed from a celebration into a—well, he wasn't quite sure what. He just knew it wouldn't be pleasant.

Hank Adamson, 48, was chief executive officer of RightNow!, a retail chain specializing in off-price clothing for young, fashion-minded women. Frankly, he had been looking forward to a little celebration. Five years ago, his company had bought out a stodgy, 20-year-old retailer of women's apparel, and Hank had come in to run the place. He renamed it and repositioned it, giving it a hip, edgy style. (*Get Your Clothes Half Off* was the latest slogan, with a racy ad campaign to match.) He invested in rapid growth: RightNow! today had stores in 28 states, with more on the way. Last year, Hank had hired a dozen or so tech-savvy 20-somethings and charged them with creating a killer Web site. Launched just last month, the site was already winning awards and generating substantial business. He'd heard that even the folks in corporate were impressed.

But oh, those 20-somethings. One in particular: Treece McDavitt. Hank had noticed her—you could hardly miss the elaborate tattoos and double eyebrow rings—but he hadn't really known her name. Until yesterday.

"We think it was Treece," Charlie Herald had told him. "It was her last day, and this was her parting shot. Not that we could pin anything on her—she covered her tracks pretty well."

Charlie, RightNow!'s VP of human resources, recounted the story as best as he had been able to piece it together. Treece was hip and edgy herself, a 26-year-old rebel without much of a cause, valuable for her many skills, but not exactly a candidate for Team Player of the Month. Evidently, she had been listening to lunchroom conversations about salaries and had heard all the usual speculation and innuendo about who made what. But where most people just gossiped and let it go, Treece got hot under the collar. She suspected unfairness. She was put out because she and her coworkers knew so little.

"Why shouldn't we know what everyone makes?" she had blurted out one day to her lunchtime companions. "I'll bet there are all kinds of disparities." Everyone laughed and agreed, plunging into irreverent comparisons of what they imagined various managers were paid. One recounted an old IBM commercial in which a malevolent computer hacker e-mails his company's payroll information to all his colleagues.

Treece had smiled. And then the conversation had gone on to other things.

Today, two months later, life was imitating Madison Avenue all too closely. Treece—if it *was* Treece—may have had help from a friend (another recent departure) who worked in HR. Or she may have relied solely on her own considerable computer skills. Whatever, as she herself might have said. No one seemed to think that Treece was a malevolent employee. "Just mischievous," one person said. But it hardly mattered. Even as she made plans to leave the company, she somehow got access to HR's files.

Yesterday was her last day, marked by a small farewell gathering and a few cupcakes. This morning, every RightNow! headquarters employee came in to work to find a camouflaged e-mail waiting on his or her computer. The e-mail bore an attachment, which listed the current salary and most recent bonus of every one of the 165 people who worked in the building.

When Hank had arrived a little after 8:30, Charlie was waiting for him. The vice president got the CEO a cup of black coffee and briefed him. Hank listened but wasn't unduly concerned. "So what?" he had said with a shrug. Everybody talks about money—they always have, always will. Chances are, everybody at the company already has a good idea of what everybody else is making. "Is this really a problem?" he remembered himself asking.

Charlie had looked straight at him. "It's 8:30 in the morning," he said evenly. "I already have four voice mails asking for appointments. I have to think people have something on their minds." Hank asked Charlie to take some soundings around the company, and the two agreed to touch base in the afternoon.

But Hank was talking with store managers all day, and it was five o'clock before Charlie could finally catch him without a phone tucked under his ear. As

---

"Some were teed off because they felt they were earning too little. But others were mortified because now everybody could see they were making more than their buddies."

Charlie walked in to Hank's office, Harriet Duval followed. Harriet was RightNow!'s chief financial officer. She and Charlie were Hank's top advisers. As they bustled in, a tune popped into Hank's head and he suppressed a chuckle. Harriet and Charlie always made him think of the line about Iowans from the old show *The Music Man*: they could stand touching noses for a week at a time and never see eye to eye. Harriet and Charlie didn't come from Iowa, so far as Hank knew, but the description did fit—which, of course, was one reason he found them both so valuable.

Charlie looked haggard. "It's worse than we thought," he said. Hank raised an eyebrow; Charlie went on, glumly. "Seems like nobody's been talking about anything else. If you had walked the halls today, you'd have seen little groups all over. People are furious! My assistant Tammy says she's never heard so much griping. And you know those voice mails I mentioned? I must have had a dozen people in my office today, every one of them upset over salaries."

Suddenly reflective, he added: "Funny thing—some were teed off because they felt they were earning too little. You'd expect that, right? But others were mortified because now everybody could see they were making more than their buddies. They wanted to know how to handle it."

Harriet nodded. "For once, I have to agree with Charlie. People are really upset. Heaven knows I've fielded my share of complaints today. At the same time, though, I have to believe it'll blow over in a day or so."

Charlie shook his head. "I don't think so. People get crazy when it comes to money—that's why this company and nearly every other company in the world keep salaries confidential. We're all scared of the reaction. Just today, four or five people actually threatened to walk. One guy even wanted another 30 grand!"

Hank started to ask a question, but Charlie held up a hand.

"Wait," he continued. "You need to know the whole story, and it gets worse. You both know how tight the job market has been recently, especially for marketers experienced in this business. We've had to pay top dollar—and now everybody in the company knows that our four new hires in marketing make more than people who've been around for years." He paused for effect. "And it really doesn't help that three of the four new marketers are men in a department that's almost all female. Can you say 'lawsuit'?"

His listeners winced. "But it isn't just in marketing, it's all over. In the dot-com group, some of those 23-year-olds make north of $50,000. That doesn't look so great to an old-timer in HR who's pulling down $42,000. As for IT, well, don't even go there. We hired that Russian programmer, Arkady, a few years ago at $38,000. He was ecstatic to get the job and is anything but a squeaky wheel when it comes to pay, so he's had only a couple of increases since then. Meanwhile, we bring that young guy Josh in to do the same work. He knows he's good, and he makes sure you know it. He negotiated a high salary when he came on, and he's been relentless in pushing for raises ever since. Now he's making $75,000."

Hank and Harriet sat silent. Harriet reflected uneasily on how her controller—loyal, quiet Edith, who had been at the company more than 20 years—now knew that her salary was less than one-third of Harriet's. Hank thought of Allan, his brother's pal, who was laid off from a much larger apparel chain. To placate his brother, Hank had hired Allan to head up store relations and had matched his big-company salary. It was far more than what RightNow! would otherwise have paid.

And oh, yes: there was Max, Hank's golfing buddy, who was hired as director of international marketing. Max was a great guy. His wife and Hank's wife were close friends. On the job, he tried hard, but he never got the kind of results a savvier, more aggressive marketer might have achieved. His boss had never given him much in the way of raises, so he earned significantly less than others at his level. Now he—and everyone else—knew it.

Finally Hank spoke: "So we've got a real mess on our hands. And I guess I'm as much to blame as anybody. We've had to add so many people in the last couple of years. I've always told Charlie, 'Get 'em in here. Pay them whatever it takes.'" He thought about mentioning Allan but then decided against it. "And I guess there have been cases where we haven't brought the lower end up fast enough." Charlie nodded tiredly.

"But wait," Harriet said. "Are we really so different from other companies? Everywhere I've worked, there have been pretty big pay disparities. The fact is, you can't really avoid it these days. You have to pay for hot skills—and you have to pay what the market dictates."

"But other companies haven't had their salaries released to the world," Hank said. "And now we're facing this staff meeting tomorrow with 165 teed-off people. Any thoughts about what I should say? Better yet, any thoughts about what we should *do*?"

"Tell them we're going to keep making the salaries public. That we're going to post them." The speaker was Charlie.

Hank and Harriet smiled, ready to laugh at the joke. But Charlie wasn't joking. He was staring at a spot on the floor, his brow furrowed. Suddenly he looked up. "I mean it. I've heard of a couple companies that do this. I think they're on to something."

Now Harriet was incredulous. "Are you nuts? This stuff going public is what's causing all the trouble! A fire breaks out and we're going to douse it with gasoline?"

"Bear with me—the idea isn't as crazy as it sounds." Charlie began to tick off his points on his fingers.

"For starters, consider how hard it is to keep salary information secret anymore. It's all out there in cyberspace, available to anyone smart enough to get it. Think there won't be another Treece?

"Point two. It would keep us honest. We've let our compensation system get out of control. You're right,

Harriet: it happens all over. But that's no excuse. Put salaries up on the board, and you can bet the employees will help us make sure they're fair."

Harriet started to argue, but Charlie plowed ahead. "But the real argument is that it helps—heck, it forces—people to understand our business. We've always said we wanted employees to understand our costs and learn to think like businesspeople. Well, here in headquarters our biggest cost is payroll. You should have heard one of the conversations I eavesdropped on today. Somebody was grousing about what we pay the dot-com kids, and two other people jumped all over him. 'Do you know how important those kids are to our future? Do you know what they could earn at one of those IT consulting companies?' Those guys were thinking like CEOs. They shut the complainer right up.

"Besides." Charlie allowed himself a small smile. "You gotta admit that we'd be cutting edge—a sure bet for a story in some big business magazine. Our name in lights."

Harriet rolled her eyes. "Charlie, you aren't thinking straight. You said it yourself—people get crazy over money. Do you really want us to spend all our time explaining to Arkady why he makes so much less than Josh?"

"But that's my point," Charlie retorted. "He shouldn't make so much less. I know—we pay for performance. But is Arkady's performance really only half as valuable as Josh's? If it is, by the way, we should fire him."

"Oh, come off it. You wouldn't even be thinking about their pay if it weren't for the mess we're in right now," Harriet charged.

"Maybe not," Charlie agreed. "But I'm working on the 'you get a lemon, you make lemonade' approach. Sure, we have to say we messed up, we'll be reviewing

---

We're dealing with real people here, and where there are people, there are egos. The problem isn't the disparities that *aren't* justified; it's the ones that *are*.

---

salaries, the usual blah blah blah. But what if we also say that we think of our employees as partners in the business and that we'll entrust them with the same information every senior manager already has access to—that is, what people make. It'd knock their socks off."

"And make them *very* nervous," Hank interjected.

"Nope. *Yesterday* it would have made them nervous," Charlie replied. "Today they already know the numbers. Now our job is to turn that into something positive."

Harriet shook her head. She had a quick tongue, everybody knew, but she was unusual in her ability to cool off, gather her arguments, then disagree calmly and rationally, without putting people on the defensive. "Charlie, it's a great idea—in theory. But we're dealing with real people here, and where there are people, there are egos. The problem isn't the disparities that *aren't* justified; it's the ones that *are*. We can fix the Arkady-Josh problem. But do we really want to tell Max—sorry, Hank, I know you're friends—that he isn't making more money because he's awkward with clients? Or what about your own assistant Tammy? You know she gets a lot more than anybody else on the support staff, partly because she's always there when some young kid has a problem. She's probably talked a dozen of them out of leaving. If we try to explain that, you can just hear the other AAs." She mimicked a petulant young administrative assistant: "'Well, that's not in *my* job description.'"

The CFO leaned back in her chair, thoughtful. "All those differences in pay—they're the result of stuff you could never talk about out loud. They reflect a hundred judgment calls that every manager makes about every employee every day. You couldn't explain them, so you wouldn't try. Instead you'd run the business like the postal service, paying everybody at a certain grade the same. Or you'd increase everybody's pay with age, like in Japan. Maybe that's okay for the government or for the Japanese, but no business in this hypercompetitive U.S. marketplace could afford it. Our best people wouldn't stand for it."

"Straw man, Harriet." Charlie's tone was earnest. "We're not the post office, and I'm not against differences in pay. I just want reasonable differences." He turned toward Hank. "Look," he said. "This is a people business. We're only as good as our buyers, our marketers, our programmers, even our support staff. And there's this awkward thing about people—they have feelings. People don't care what the market says about what they should be paid; they care what the company says—and they *really* care how much they make compared with the guy in the next office. If they don't feel fairly treated, they get sullen. They do bad things, like leave at five o'clock when there's still work to be done. Or just leave, period."

"You talk like there's some kind of fairness that everybody agrees on," Harriet retorted. "There isn't. People feel it's fair if they earn more than the guy in the next cube. But do you really know anybody who thinks it's fair if they earn less? And now you want to rub their noses in the unfairness? Or have us spend all our time trying to explain it?"

She, too, turned to the CEO. "Hank, Charlie's heart is in the right place, except that it seems to have taken over his brain. Do what he suggests and we're just asking for trouble. At the meeting tomorrow, you should listen sympathetically. You should make all the right noises about conducting a review, examining disparities, and so on. And we should do that, of course; we need to get our compensation system in order. But then we should beef up our computer security so that this never happens again and go about our business. People will continue to gossip for a while. But they'll eventually forget about it."

The two stood up, and Hank thanked them as they left the office. And then he began thinking, and thinking some more, until the sky outside his window turned dark. Charlie's idea? Outlandish, no doubt. But some of his arguments weren't totally crazy, particularly the notion that this would probably happen again sometime. Even if the company didn't post salaries, maybe it could find some middle ground. An employee committee to advise them on salaries? Posting payroll costs by department, with no individual listings? Posting salaries by position, but with no names attached? Hank knew Harriet wouldn't buy any of this. And maybe she was right. Maybe it would all go away.

But maybe they were missing an opportunity, as Charlie believed.

And just how mad were all those employees likely to be at the staff meeting tomorrow? Hank didn't want to make them madder.

Now the night outside was lit only by a crescent moon and those relentless orange lights. The CEO continued to gaze out the window.

What Should Hank Do About the Salary Debacle?

Four commentators offer their advice.

➤ Victor Sim

Victor Sim is the vice president of total compensation at Prudential Insurance Company of America in Newark, New Jersey.

I can understand what Hank Adamson's going through because, in a roundabout way, I've been there. My advice to him would be to act but not overreact. Overreacting could create problems that will be difficult to live with later. For one thing, he shouldn't follow Charlie Herald's advice and publish everyone's salary. That would negatively affect employees' privacy and RightNow!'s ability to compete for talent.

Let me explain why I feel for Hank. As a mutual insurance company, Prudential for years has been required to file with the New York superintendent of insurance the name, title, and compensation of all employees making more than $60,000. The law was designed to disclose the salaries of top executives, as an anticorruption measure to protect policyholders. But over the years, as salaries rose and the law wasn't updated, it in fact applied to a large portion of the workforce.

For a long time, it didn't matter much, even though someone could get all the data from the insurance department. But with the advent of the personal computer and e-mail, it suddenly became much easier to organize and circulate salary information. Then last year, someone posted all the salaries on the Internet. In response, we, along with other insurance companies, asked the insurance department to change its practice by posting the salary for each job but, except in the case of top executives, with no individuals' names attached. Because there are dozens if not hundreds of people in most job categories, anonymity for most people was ensured when the insurance department agreed to our request.

Why did we push for the change? First, there's a personal privacy issue. People who join Prudential don't want their salary information made available to neighbors and friends. In the case of RightNow!, there's no need to add insult to injury for someone like Max, Hank's golfing buddy, who is making less than his colleagues. Second, there's a corporate competition issue. Having the compensation of all employees disclosed in the marketplace makes the company more vulnerable to poaching. Competitors can target individuals, knowing what kinds of salaries they need to offer. The same thing could happen if, as Charlie proposes, RightNow! were to post all names and salaries on a company bulletin board.

Still, Hank needs to acknowledge to his employees that the company's compensation practices need improvement. He should then establish a professionally designed compensation system—one with defined pay grades and salary ranges for each grade. Employees should be involved in the development of the system, contributing ideas on the salary ranges of different jobs and on how merit is actually measured. And the system should be open so that employees know their salary range and have a clear idea of where their job fits into the company's pay structure.

This would allow employees to see how they're being treated relative to others in the company. Without that openness, people end up comparing themselves against the salaries, real or imagined, of other individuals. This raises all kinds of emotional issues. And you're never going to convince everyone that they're being treated fairly in a one-to-one comparison unless you are willing to unearth the nitty-gritty details of each salary decision and air the dirty laundry of every employee.

One frequently cited problem of such a formal pay structure is that it doesn't allow for flexibility in a tight job market, where you typically need to pay a recruitment premium above a job's market value to attract people. One way to avoid paying such a premium, and to maintain the fairness of your salary structure, is to recruit individuals who you believe are ready for the job but have not yet been promoted to an equivalent job in their own companies. For example, a vice president who has been groomed for a senior vice president position at another company, but is waiting for a position to open, may jump at the chance to fill your opening for a senior VP. "Value hiring," like value investing, allows you to pick up bargains, if you will, and pay the market value of the job you are filling.

➤ Dennis Bakke

Dennis Bakke is the CEO of AES Corporation, a $6.7 billion global electricity company based in Arlington, Virginia. He and AES chairman Roger Sant were the subject of the HBR interview "Organizing for Empowerment" (January–February, 1999).

With all due respect to Charlie, Hank should start by eliminating the entire HR department: compensation should be in the hands of the employees themselves and their leaders, not some staff group. He should eliminate all salary guidelines and publish everyone's pay. And he should require managers to collect input from others before setting an employee's compensation.

To put this in perspective, you must realize that AES has a fairly unconventional approach to managing people. Our electricity plants and distribution companies around the world—and our 53,000 employees—have a lot of autonomy. We don't have any public relations, human resources, or planning departments in the home office or in individual business units. About the only rule we have is that whenever people make important decisions, they have to seek—though not necessarily follow—at least one other employee's advice. We do what we can to encourage an open and honest environment.

At the same time, I have to be honest: 14 years ago, Roger Sant and I suggested to our business managers that they publish people's salaries. I don't think any of them took our advice. The managers basically said that that they didn't want to have to explain salary differences to every single employee. Over the years, some of the younger managers have started sharing more salary information. Although such openness is more difficult for managers, I believe it leads to a healthier work environment. You should indeed have a reason for the salary you set for each individual employee—and be willing and able to justify the differences.

Critics will say that an open-salary system constrains you from paying what is necessary to attract and retain the best people. But perhaps you shouldn't be using money as a weapon in the fight for talent. In AES's early days, I asked people I was recruiting to take a pay cut—not because they didn't deserve the money but because I didn't want money to be the reason people were coming on board. I want them to join because they value an environment where they can use all their gifts and skills without being squelched.

Conversely, we don't have a long vesting period for options because we don't want to set up fences to keep people here one minute longer than they want to be. It's the work environment—not the salary structure—that people ought to be thinking about. Make your company a rewarding and engaging and exciting place to work, and pay issues become far less consequential.

But, you might ask, aren't job categories and guidelines necessary in order to ensure fairness? My feeling is that the entire area of compensation is overmanaged. At AES, we have no salary grades. We don't try to pigeonhole a person's unique abilities and accomplishments into a job category.

Instead, before AES managers set the compensation of direct reports, they solicit feedback from other managers within their group and across the company—and often get the advice of the person whose compensation they are determining. Responses range from "Boy, that seems a little too high" to "Why is this bonus so low?" That shared information gives people a chance to ensure there's some consistency and fairness across and within groups.

I should add that, while most of our businesses still do not publish salaries, we have a plant in Pennsylvania where employees just started setting their own individual salaries. We had tried this in the past and it was a disaster: the good workers set them far too low, and the bad ones set them far too high. But in the most recent case, the group followed our rule of getting advice before making any decision. So the individual employee, before setting his own salary, had to circulate his proposed compensation and get comments from his boss and colleagues. And the plant came in with salaries that were within budget. It's fascinating what you can do without an HR department.

➢ Ira Kay

Ira Kay directs the compensation consulting practice at Watson Wyatt Worldwide, which advises companies on employee benefits, human resources technologies, and human capital management. He is based in New York City.

The delicate and challenging situation Hank faces could prove to be a big opportunity if he looks at it the right way and understands that his choice is not strictly about compensation policy but about corporate culture. Hank has a chance to embrace a more open culture at RightNow!—one that can have the positive effect of boosting the company's financial performance.

Maintaining a relatively transparent salary structure falls into that category of corporate behaviors—eliminating executive parking spaces, involving lots of people in hiring, limiting the use of titles—that can contribute to a collegial and open work environment. Research we have done at Watson Wyatt indicates that companies with such an environment have higher returns to shareholders because they are typically more innovative and entrepreneurial.

Now that doesn't mean you should reveal everyone's salary, which would undermine the efforts of a fast-growing company like RightNow! to attract talent in a tight job market. If you're going to publish everyone's salary, you need to have internal equity—that is, similar pay for people with similar experience doing similar jobs. And internal equity usually clashes with paying people their external market value. After all, if you hire people from outside the company, you'll typically have to offer them 20% to 25% more than what they currently make—and, in all likelihood, more than what their counterparts in your own company make.

You could change your hiring strategy and promote people solely from within, recruiting them out of college, training them, and moving them up the ranks. But when you're growing rapidly, that isn't possible. Consequently, in the booming economy of the past five years or so, internal equity has given way in most companies to the need to recruit and retain sufficient numbers of the right people. In such a situation, you simply can't have an open-book salary policy.

Harriet Duval is absolutely right: if you have to pay new hires 25% more than people who are already in the same jobs, you can't rub people's faces in that. Nor can you immediately raise everybody's salary to match the new recruits' salaries. You'll simply destroy your margins.

But now that the cat's out of the bag at RightNow!, Hank has to act. A good managerial compromise, and a step toward the open culture that can enhance financial performance, would be to publish the salary ranges—or "bands"—for all of the jobs within the company. Each band will have enough variation to absorb most labor-market or individual-performance differences. High performers who are recruited from the outside might initially be paid above their salary band. But the goal would be to bring everyone within the band, typically by letting the band, and those within it, catch up with the higher paid employees over time.

Publishing salary bands lets people know how their pay compares with others' in the same job and what their jobs are worth relative to others in the company. It lets them know the upside potential of their current job and their career opportunities within the company—all job openings should be disclosed to employees on the corporate intranet—without telling them what everyone else makes. Employees should be treated like adults, with access to as much company information as possible. But some information is just too personal to disclose.

The publication of salary bands is only one of the moves that Hank should make to establish a more open culture. Taken as a whole, these measures would create an environment of trust and collegiality that, interestingly, might ultimately allow RightNow! to adopt Charlie's open-book proposal.

People can build a career at a collegial company in a way that often isn't possible at a place that hires mercenaries from the open market and spits out those who are having short-term performance difficulties. The psychological compensation that comes from working in a supportive environment of long-term commitment might make up for the slightly lower pay that would result from an open-book salary policy.

➤ Bruce Tulgan

Bruce Tulgan is the author of Winning the Talent Wars *(W.W. Norton, 2001) and* Managing Generation X *(W.W. Norton, 2000). He is also the founder of Rainmaker Thinking, a management consulting firm based in New Haven, Connecticut.*

Hank is being forced to face the difficult issue of whether to make employee compensation transparent. But what he—and every CEO—should also be considering is something much more radical: whether employees' pay, like contractors' pay, should be negotiated based on the project and the value of the work being done.

Hank must realize the futility of trying to maintain salary secrecy in today's information environment. Countless Web sites let employees examine salary surveys throughout entire industries. Individuals can also test their own true market value through the now common practice of continuous job shopping. What's more, this job shopping can be done in a low-risk manner at job-search and talent-auction Web sites.

Charlie is right to consider that another employee down the road might access compensation data and repeat Treece's e-mail mischief. But there's a more important point: top executives, supervisors, HR professionals, and accounting people have always been in the know about individuals' salaries. And people today—especially those in the workforce born after 1963, Generation X and Generation Y—are much more open about sharing and comparing pay information with their peers. With so much information swirling around today's business landscape, more speculation about compensation will occur up and down the corporate ladder. Surely, accurate information is more constructive than speculation.

Indeed, the growing availability of accurate information about the real value of workers' skills, abilities, and output is critical to making the overall labor market more fluid and more efficient. That larger economic trend is too powerful for any one employer to overlook. Employers should not buck the trend.

Without wage transparency, market pressures cannot work their true magic and ensure that compensation reflects real value. We see this in the case study. One of the main reasons that Hank and Harriet are worried about the public disclosure of salaries is that they know their company's compensation system is not entirely performance based. One solution is to make the system more rigorous so that it reflects real value.

Harriet says that even a fair system will seem unfair by employees whose feelings may be hurt. This concern is archaic and paternalistic. Employees must be sophisticated enough to understand their manager's reasoning, to negotiate on their own behalf, and to make decisions about the relative fairness of salaries. True, some employees won't succeed with that degree of pressure. But smart companies are looking for employees who respond to that pressure by becoming more valuable. And most employees won't resent compensation differentials based on ongoing transparent pay-for-performance negotiations.

Every step of the way, managers must clearly define each employee's objectives and tie rewards directly to meeting those objectives. The most important transparency factor is not whether employees know what others earn, but rather that all of them know exactly why they earn what they do and what they need to do to earn more.

Harriet and Hank make an important point when they say that intangible factors require managers to be subjective when evaluating employee performance. That's why the ongoing negotiation process is so important. The worth of one employee's work today is whatever the day's negotiation yields. That kind of real market pressure on both employers and employees will drive worker productivity through the roof.

Managers at RightNow! will have to roll up their sleeves, negotiate short-term pay-for-performance deals with every employee on every project, measure every individual's performance every day, and keep good contemporaneous records. Harriet is dead right: it's going to be an extremely high maintenance system for managers. But if you want high productivity, you have to accept high maintenance.

Originally published in May 2001

Reprint Ro105A

ABOUT THE CONTRIBUTORS

Julia Kirby is a senior editor at *Harvard Business Review*.

Nicholas G. Carr is a former executive editor at *Harvard Business Review*.

Suzy Wetlaufer is the former editor-in-chief at *Harvard Business Review*.

Sarah Cliffe is an executive editor at *Harvard Business Review*.

Gordon Adler is senior writer at IMD, the International Institute for Management Development in Lausanne, Switzerland. He is also a novelist and communications consultant and has managed an international school.

Eileen Roche is an associate editor at *Harvard Business Review*.

John Case is author of *Open-Book Management* (HarperBusiness, 1995) and *The Open-Book Experience* (Perseus, 1998), as well as several other business books. His article "Opening the Books" appeared in the March–April 1997 issue of the *Harvard Business Review*.

Harvard Business Review Paperback Series

The Harvard Business Review Paperback Series offers the best thinking on cutting-edge management ideas from the world's leading thinkers, researchers, and managers. Designed for leaders who believe in the power of ideas to change business, these books will be useful to managers at all levels of experience, but especially senior executives and general managers. In addition, this series is widely used in training and executive development programs.

Books are priced at $19.95 U.S.
Price subject to change.

Title	Product #
Harvard Business Review **Interviews with CEOs**	3294
Harvard Business Review on **Advances in Strategy**	8032
Harvard Business Review on **Becoming a High Performance Manager**	1296
Harvard Business Review on **Brand Management**	1445
Harvard Business Review on **Breakthrough Leadership**	8059
Harvard Business Review on **Breakthrough Thinking**	181X
Harvard Business Review on **Building Personal and Organizational Resilience**	2721
Harvard Business Review on **Business and the Environment**	2336
Harvard Business Review on **Change**	8842
Harvard Business Review on **Compensation**	701X
Harvard Business Review on **Corporate Ethics**	273X
Harvard Business Review on **Corporate Governance**	2379
Harvard Business Review on **Corporate Responsibility**	2748
Harvard Business Review on **Corporate Strategy**	1429
Harvard Business Review on **Crisis Management**	2352
Harvard Business Review on **Culture and Change**	8369
Harvard Business Review on **Customer Relationship Management**	6994
Harvard Business Review on **Decision Making**	5572
Harvard Business Review on **Effective Communication**	1437

Title	Product #
Harvard Business Review on **Entrepreneurship**	9105
Harvard Business Review on **Finding and Keeping the Best People**	5564
Harvard Business Review on **Innovation**	6145
Harvard Business Review on **Knowledge Management**	8818
Harvard Business Review on **Leadership**	8834
Harvard Business Review on **Leadership at the Top**	2756
Harvard Business Review on **Leading in Turbulent Times**	1806
Harvard Business Review on **Managing Diversity**	7001
Harvard Business Review on **Managing High-Tech Industries**	1828
Harvard Business Review on **Managing People**	9075
Harvard Business Review on **Managing the Value Chain**	2344
Harvard Business Review on **Managing Uncertainty**	9083
Harvard Business Review on **Managing Your Career**	1318
Harvard Business Review on **Marketing**	8040
Harvard Business Review on **Measuring Corporate Performance**	8826
Harvard Business Review on **Mergers and Acquisitions**	5556
Harvard Business Review on **Motivating People**	1326
Harvard Business Review on **Negotiation**	2360
Harvard Business Review on **Nonprofits**	9091
Harvard Business Review on **Organizational Learning**	6153
Harvard Business Review on **Strategic Alliances**	1334
Harvard Business Review on **Strategies for Growth**	8850
Harvard Business Review on **The Business Value of IT**	9121
Harvard Business Review on **The Innovative Enterprise**	130X
Harvard Business Review on **Turnarounds**	6366
Harvard Business Review on **What Makes a Leader**	6374
Harvard Business Review on **Work and Life Balance**	3286

Harvard Business Essentials

In the fast-paced world of business today, everyone needs a personal resource—a place to go for advice, coaching, background information, or answers. The Harvard Business Essentials series fits the bill. Concise and straightforward, these books provide highly practical advice for readers at all levels of experience. Whether you are a new manager interested in expanding your skills or an experienced executive looking to stay on top, these solution-oriented books give you the reliable tips and tools you need to improve your performance and get the job done. Harvard Business Essentials titles will quickly become your constant companions and trusted guides.

These books are priced at $19.95 U.S., except as noted.
Price subject to change.

Title	Product #
Harvard Business Essentials: **Negotiation**	1113
Harvard Business Essentials: **Managing Creativity and Innovation**	1121
Harvard Business Essentials: **Managing Change and Transition**	8741
Harvard Business Essentials: **Hiring and Keeping the Best People**	875X
Harvard Business Essentials: **Finance**	8768
Harvard Business Essentials: **Business Communication**	113X
Harvard Business Essentials: **Manager's Toolkit ($24.95)**	2896
Harvard Business Essentials: **Managing Projects Large and Small**	3213
Harvard Business Essentials: **Creating Teams with an Edge**	290X

To order, call 1-800-668-6780, or go online at www.HBSPress.org

The Results-Driven Manager

The Results-Driven Manager series collects timely articles from *Harvard Management Update* and *Harvard Management Communication Letter* to help senior to middle managers sharpen their skills, increase their effectiveness, and gain a competitive edge. Presented in a concise, accessible format to save managers valuable time, these books offer authoritative insights and techniques for improving job performance and achieving immediate results.

These books are priced at $14.95 U.S.
Price subject to change.

To order, call 1-800-668-6780, or go online at www.HBSPress.org

Management Dilemmas: Case Studies from the Pages of Harvard Business Review

How often do you wish you could turn to a panel of experts to guide you through tough management situations? The Management Dilemmas series provides just that. Drawn from the pages of *Harvard Business Review*, each insightful volume poses several perplexing predicaments and shares the problem-solving wisdom of leading experts. Engagingly written, these solutions-oriented collections help managers make sound judgment calls when addressing everyday management dilemmas.

These books are priced at $19.95 U.S.
Price subject to change.

Title	Product #
Management Dilemmas: **When Change Comes Undone**	5038
Management Dilemmas: **When Good People Behave Badly**	5046
Management Dilemmas: **When Marketing Becomes a Minefield**	290X

Readers of the Management Dilemmas series find the following Harvard Business School Press books of interest.

If you find these books useful:	You may also like these:
When Change Comes Undone	Leading Change (7471)
	The Heart of Change (2549)
When Good People Behave Badly	Toxic Emotions at Work (2573)
	The Set-Up-to-Fail Syndrome (9490)
When Marketing Becomes a Minefield	How Customers Think (8261)
	Marketing Moves (6005)
	United We Brand (7982)

To order, call 1-800-668-6780, or go online at www.HBSPress.org

How to Order

Harvard Business School Press publications are available worldwide
from your local bookseller or online retailer.
You can also call

1-800-668-6780

Our product consultants are available to help you
8:00 a.m.–6:00 p.m., Monday–Friday, Eastern Time.
Outside the U.S. and Canada, call: 617-783-7450
Please call about special discounts for quantities greater than ten.

You can order online at

www.HBSPress.org